Faithful Listening

Discernment in Everyday Life

Joan Mueller, Ph.D.

SHEED & WARD

Lanham, Chicago, New York, Toronto, and Oxford

To those who have mentored me in discernment,

Margaret Halaska, OSF

Jules Toner, S.J.

Bert Thelen, S.J.

Published by Sheed & Ward
An imprint of Rowman & Littlefield Publishers, Inc.
A wholly owned subsidiary of The Rowman & Littlefield Publishing Group, Inc.
4501 Forbes Boulevard, Suite 200
Lanham, MD 20706

PO Box 317
Oxford
OX2 9RU, UK

Library of Congress Cataloging-in-Publication Data

Mueller, Joan, 1956–
    Faithful listening : discernment in everyday life / Joan Mueller.
        p. cm.
    Includes bibliographical references.
    ISBN 1-55612-900-9 (alk. paper)
    1. Spiritual life—Catholic Church. 2. Discernment of spirits. 3. Ignatius of Loyola,
Saint, 1491–1556. I. Title.
    BX2350.2.M79   1996
    248.4'6—dc20   96-9153

Printed in the United States of America.

⊖™ The paper used in this publication meets the minimum requirements of
American National Standard for Information Sciences—Permanence of
Paper for Printed Library Materials, ANSI/NISO Z39.48-1992.

Contents

Acknowledgments

Grateful acknowledgment is given for copyright reprint permissions as follows:

Exerpts from Ignatius of Loyola are taken from *Spiritual Exercises and Selected Works*, George E. Ganss, SJ, ed. Copyright© 1991 by Paulist Press. Used by permission.

Exerpts from St. Teresa of Avila are taken from *The Interior Castle*, Kieran Kavanaugh, OCD and Otilio Rodriguez, OCD, trans. Copyright© 1979 by Paulist Press. Used by permission.

Excerpts from Athanasius are taken from *The Life of Antony and the Letter to Marcellinus*, Robert C. Gregg, trans. Copyright© 1980 by Paulist Press. Used by permission.

Excerpts from Francis and Clare are taken from *The Complete Works*, Regis J. Armstrong, OFM and Ignatius C. Brady, OFM, trans. Copyright© 1982 by Paulist Press. Used by permission.

Excerpts from *The Screwtape Letters* by C.S. Lewis, copyright© by HarperCollins Publishers Limited. Used by permission.

Excerpts from "With God and a Medical Kit in the Mountains" are taken from *El Salvador: A Spring Whose Waters Never Run Dry*, Scott Wright, Minor Sinclair, Margaret Lyle and David Scott, eds. Copyright© 1990 by the Ecumenical Program on Central America and the Caribbean. Used by permission.

Excerpts from St. John of the Cross are taken from *The Collected Works of St. John of the Cross*, translated by Kieran Kavanaugh and Otilio Rodriguez. Copyright© 1979, 1991 by Washington Province of Discalced Carmelites. ICS Publications, 2131 Lincoln Road N.E., Washington, DC 20002, USA. Used by permission.

Excerpts from *Mirror of Perfection*, Leo Sherley-Price, ed., are taken from *St. Francis of Assisi: Writings and Early Biographies*, Marion A. Habig, ed. Copyright© 1973 by Franciscan Herald Press. Used by permission.

Preface

Western Christianity often neglects the Holy Spirit. The role of the Holy Spirit in Christian life is frequently confined to prayers before tests, confirmation classes and charismatic prayer meetings. Many Christians find it difficult to imagine themselves having a relationship with the Spirit of God that intimately shapes their daily lives.

On the other hand, when listening to people speak of their everyday faith, one hears many stories of Christians who truly do love the Spirit of God. Some work to foster a spirit of cooperation and peace at work, in a classroom or at the office. Others teach their children that a spirit of love and respect is essential for a mature life. Still others offer a spirit of generosity and self-forgetfulness in their service to the poor, the uneducated or the oppressed.

This book explores how one might deepen one's personal relationship with the Holy Spirit. By pondering the mystery of the Spirit of God in the midst of daily life, it is hoped that Christians can identify their own love for the Holy Spirit and will strive to be more faithful in this love. Perhaps learning to discern the presence of the Spirit in daily life will help Christians use discernment more effectively in their congregations and parishes.

This book is not meant to be simply read. It is intended to be pondered, prayed and discussed with others. Discussion questions, role-plays and case studies are part of the process of this book. Those who use it within the context of a class or faith-sharing group will probably reap its fullest benefits. Case studies have been written with a particular sensitivity to cultural and socioeconomic diversity.

Many people have contributed to this project. Over the years, my discernment classes in the Creighton Spirituality Program have fueled my scholarly interest in this topic and have refined my presentations and method. While I was writing this book, twelve students taking a class in discernment: Kathy Ponce, Mary Carian, Linda Kemeny, OSF, Chris Deily, Bev Deprey, Alana Gorski, OSF, Mary Kaminski, Marion Lopina, Melanie Paradis, OSF, Carlene Larson, Rob Quirk, SDS, and Marie Scott, CSA, most of whom are involved in pastoral work, critiqued drafts of the chapters. Their comments and insights were invaluable. My good friend, Joanne Meyer, OSF, proofread most of the text. Her critique coupled careful logic with tender pastoral sense. To her I am most grateful.

I requested the aid of many people when writing the case studies included in this text. I deeply appreciate the wisdom of Coletta Dunn, OSF, and Sheila Haskett, OSF, in the case of Tony; the cultural sensitivity of Cecilia Canales, OP, Christine Morkozsky, CDP, and Lucille Flores, SSM, in the case of Carmen; the advice Shawnee Sykes, SSND, gave me to "say it like it is" in the case of the Christian Women Society; and the pastoral sensitivity of Francis Dombrowski, OFM, Cap., who affirmed me in the case of Jerry.

Colleagues who support one in a project such as this are especially valued. Dennis Sylva, Ph.D., and Joan Cook, SC, graciously offered their scholarly insights on discernment in prophetic literature. Margarett Schlientz, Ph.D. opened her basement office and fed me soup twice a day so that I could finish the final draft of this text over a Christmas break. I was very touched when Kieran Kavanaugh, OCD, translated and faxed background information to me on Saint John of the Cross' letter to a Carmelite nun. Such kindness was more than I expected.

Finally I wish to thank my friend, Jules Toner, S.J., who continues to dedicate his life to the study of discernment. Nine years ago, I spent a year praying and pondering Fr. Toner's *Commentary*. Since then I continue to grow in love and respect for Fr. Toner. This text is indebted to his work.

Joan Mueller, Ph.D.

∂ About the Author ∂

Joan Mueller, Ph.D., Assistant Professor of Theology at Creighton University, received her Ph.D. in Systematic Theology from Duquesne University. She is the author of Why I Can't Forgive You: A Christian Reflection *(Thomas More, 1996).*

1

The Search for a
Discerning Lifestyle

Reflecting Upon Discernment Experiences

Everyone is discerning these days. Young people are encouraged to discern carefully their vocation in life. Seminar leaders are teaching discernment. Religious men and women attend chapters to discern new leadership. Parishioners are asked to participate in discernment processes.

Though there is renewed interest in discernment among Christians, it is difficult to determine exactly what discernment means. Neither the spiritual tradition nor contemporary experience offers a well-formulated definition. It is commonly suggested that discernment is a means by which an individual discovers the will of God. Processes aimed at developing consensus within religious organizations are often termed "discernment processes." At times, the term "discernment" refers to the virtue of discretion. Discernment can be proposed as a style of ecclesial organization. It can also be thought of as a process by which people distinguish moods, emotions, tendencies, inclinations and events leading them toward God from those leading them away from God. Given all these meanings, it is not surprising to discover that people who speak about discernment are not using the word uniformly.

When a word is rich in experience and tradition, one discovers its meaning most effectively if one thinks of it not as a definition to be conquered but as a mystery to be con-

1

templated. "Marriage" is such a word. Marriage can be imaged as a legal contract, a sacred covenant, a sign of Christ's love for the church, a ritual symbolizing the union of a couple, a context of generative love, etc. All these images held together in creative tension reveal the unending nuances and challenges of the mystery of married love. The context by which one learns this creative tension is found not in clear textbook definitions, but in daily fidelity to married life.

Discernment is also a mystery. Christians broadly refer to the mystery of discernment as the God-given desire to listen to God by following the Spirit of Jesus present within daily life. One grows in this gift of discernment through fidelity to a discerning lifestyle. Such a lifestyle demands trust, includes failure and matures through self-reflection and prayer.

Prayerfully begging God for the gift of discernment and reflecting upon one's experiences of discerning can encourage growth in a discerning lifestyle. What measure might one use to guide this reflection? In his letter to the Galatians, St. Paul teaches the Christian community how they might discern their experiences. He suggests that the Galatians look at the fruits of their dealings with God and others. While the Holy Spirit produces good fruits such as love, joy, peace, patience, kindness, generosity, faithfulness, gentleness and self-control (Gal 5:22-23), an opposing spirit produces division, bickering and immoral conduct (Gal 5:17-21). In other passages, Paul proposes other distinguishing fruits of the Holy Spirit. Some of these fruits are order (1 Cor 14:32-33), freedom (Gal 4:12-31), unity (Eph 4:1-6), intelligent orthodoxy (1 Tim 1:3-7; 2 Tim 3:1-9), thanksgiving and praise (Eph 5:18-20) and forgiveness (Eph 4:30-32; 2 Cor 2:5-11).

While discerning the fruits of the Holy Spirit is an effective guide to the art of self-reflection, discerning the fruits is only one of many possible tools that Christians might use. Traditionally, Christians have reviewed their experiences through the lenses of common sense, scripture and tradition. Often Christians have found a spiritual guide familiar with the living of Christian discernment to help them in this process.

To demonstrate reflection guided by common sense, scripture and tradition, four contemporary case studies of good people entering into discernment processes are given below. As you reflect upon each case, try to apply St. Paul's method of distinguishing between the fruits. Questions are inserted to encourage the reader to ponder the experience from perspectives derived from common sense, scripture and tradition. A sample analysis is offered after each case.

Contemporary Discernment Cases

Case One: The Construction Project

The Case

A religious superior asked her community to attend a "discernment meeting" regarding the future use of a building that until recently had housed a school sponsored by the community. The sisters were under the impression that the purpose of the meeting was to propose ideas for the vacant building. Before convening the meeting, the Community Director, who was to her credit quite gifted at restoring old community buildings into environments for contemporary ministry, formulated a plan to renovate the building into a neighborhood apartment complex.

After considerable research, the Community Director became convinced that her plan would be service-oriented and profitable for the community. Since one of her more recent decisions proved disastrous and since the renovation project had the potential of financially devastating the community, she knew she needed the support of the sisters.

The meeting began with the introduction of a nationally known facilitator who was groomed to lead the sisters through the process. The Community Director's plan was presented and the question for discernment was posed to the assembled body. The sisters were asked to discern whether they would give the superior complete authority to move ahead with the proposed project.

During the short period reserved for questions, some sisters dared to suggest other possible uses for the building. Since they had presupposed that the purpose of the meeting was to do initial brainstorming, their ideas were not well-formulated. The facilitator came prepared to counter opposing ideas and alternate voices were quickly silenced.

At the break, the only operative proposal was the Community Director's plan. The sisters were reminded by the facilitator that discernment involved prayer. To facilitate this needed prayer, ten minutes were allowed for prayerful consideration of the proposed plan, personal break, cookies and punch and visiting friends. The sisters took fifteen minutes and then reassembled.

In the end, the sisters modified the Community Director's request asking her to periodically report to them concerning the project's progress. The superior willingly agreed to this. In the next community newsletter, the headline stated that "consensus" had been reached concerning the renovation project. The alternate voices had not only been silenced, they had been negated.

Most sisters went home quite comfortable with the decision to support their superior. A few sisters expressed frustration at not being able to explore other options. Soon these dissenting voices became busy with their individual ministries and the project proceeded.

Questions on Case One

1. What is the role of research in discernment processes?
2. How might the Community Director have more clearly stated the issue to be discerned?

3. What do you think the role of prayer might be in a discernment process?

4. What is consensus? What role does consensus play in discernment?

5. How would you describe the fruits of this discernment process?

Analysis of Case One

Case One portrays a Community Director anxious to serve her community wisely and efficiently. The use of her gifts of planning and her desire for unity are fruits of the Spirit's presence in her life.

Although the Community Director did unite the sisters in action that proved beneficial for the community, she did so by manipulating the sister's cooperation. This kind of manipulation of others' freedom is not characteristic of the Holy Spirit. The sisters responded by recognizing the Community Director's good sense and talent, but they did not commit energy to the project other than demanding occasional reviews. Essentially the project remained the superior's project.

Some sisters left disillusioned because the topic for discernment was not clearly stated. This kind of confusion is not a fruit of the Holy Spirit. Although the sisters seemed willing to overlook this confusion, the next time the superior calls a meeting the sisters might suspect a covert agenda. Suspicion is not a fruit of the Holy Spirit. A clearly defined discernment does not invite such suspicion. When calling a group together for discernment, clarity concerning the issue to be discerned is essential.

The lip-service done to the role of prayer in this discernment process was disheartening. Since the Community Director had a predetermined agenda to sell the congregation, the necessity of fervently asking God for help and guidance did not arise. Stories from the Christian spiritual tradition demonstrate that prayer must not only be present but must permeate Christian discernment processes. While the Community Director paid close attention to fiscal realities and the possibility of dissenting voices, she failed to recognize that God was present within the assembled community of sisters. The normal spirit of thanksgiving and worship that is core to such assemblies did not happen. Something was wrong.

The Christian tradition suggests that attachment to a particular agenda or plan when entering into a discernment process is detrimental to the process.[1] While intelligent and responsible planning is necessary for discernment, personal attachment to a particular plan prohibits attentiveness to the Spirit of God. The superior fostered the acceptance of an intelligent and well-formulated proposal, but she did not facilitate a discernment process.

The following chart outlines a few insights that might be learned from Case One.

Insights Into Discernment from Case One

- **Discernment Respects the Freedom of Others**
  Manipulating cooperation is not the work of the Holy Spirit.

- **The Discernment Issue Must Be Clearly Stated**
  Participants must have clear awareness of what they are discerning.

- **Prayer Is Central to Discernment**
  If one is seeking to know the ways of God, one must fervently beg God for enlightenment, fidelity and courage. Without this prayer, one may make a decision, but one is not discerning.

Case Two: The Amalgamation of Inner City Parishes

The Case

Both the bishop and the parishioners knew that some amalgamation of resources needed to be done in the inner city. In a small area there were few parishioners, limited financial resources and ten churches. Eventually the financial situation required the bishop to initiate a decision-making process.

To calm the worries of his people, the bishop assured them that he would discern their future with them. He appointed a priest to oversee an elaborate discernment process complete with task forces, town hall meetings and prayer services.

The people volunteered their time and attended the town hall meetings and prayer services in record numbers. They elicited the help of professionals to formulate equitable and realistic options. They were faithful to the time-lines of the process and regularly reviewed their progress with the designated authorities.

Two weeks before the end of the discernment process, the people were beginning to envision what the future might hold. Although there were a few dissidents who wanted to hold on to the old ways, most of the parishioners were moving toward accepting a common plan.

Before listening to this plan, the bishop appeared unexpectedly at a town hall meeting and informed the parishioners that he had made a decision. Resources for implementing his decision were in place and a new diocesan position was created to insure a smooth beginning.

The people left the meeting shocked and angry. Some accused the bishop of racism. Others vowed that they would never trust the church again. Some old faithfuls simply reoriented themselves toward the new direction.

Questions on Case Two

1. What role might the limitations of personal and financial resources play in discerment processes?
2. What role does legitimate authority play in discernment processes?
3. What fruits are you noticing?

Analysis of Case Two

Case Two presents a well-organized, intelligent and prayerful discernment process which was first proposed and then aborted by a bishop. The result of this inconsistency was a grave betrayal of the good will of the people.

One can understand the bishop's response by recognizing that he was perhaps caught in the organizational shift required of hierarchical institutions using discernment processes. When the bishop saw his people taking responsibility for their future, he failed to trust the proposed process and panicked. The people were disillusioned by his sudden regression into authoritarianism. If discernment language is going to be used, one must trust that the Holy Spirit can truly work through people who cooperate with those in leadership positions. Authority that operates out of an authoritarian mode while using discernment language perpetrates injustice.

The dance between freedom and order is an intricate one. St. Paul suggests that the Spirit brings true order (1 Cor 14:32-33). It seemed that the people were formulating a plan that was ordered, fair and supported by those willing to enter into discernment. A glimpse of this kind of order was seen in this case.

To his credit, the bishop had proposed a well-organized and prayerful discernment process. Allowing a "free-for-all" under the guise of discernment would have been as disastrous as the bishop's regression into authoritarianism. The mystics have always recognized a role for intelligent organization and planning when speaking of discernment.

Perhaps the one who became the most impoverished in this situation was the bishop, who deprived himself of the energy and joy of the Holy Spirit working in and through his people. While holding on to his isolated authority, the bishop deprived himself of the trust and spontaneous affection of his people. Since trust is the foundation of relation-

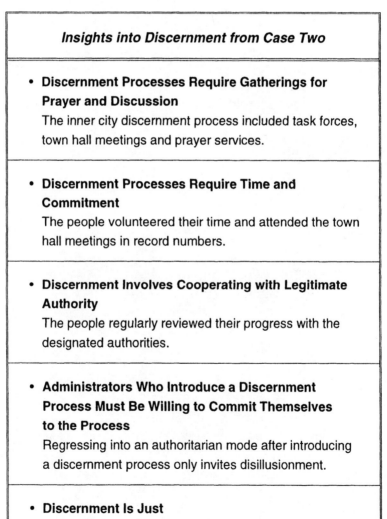

Insights into Discernment from Case Two

- **Discernment Processes Require Gatherings for Prayer and Discussion**
  The inner city discernment process included task forces, town hall meetings and prayer services.

- **Discernment Processes Require Time and Commitment**
  The people volunteered their time and attended the town hall meetings in record numbers.

- **Discernment Involves Cooperating with Legitimate Authority**
  The people regularly reviewed their progress with the designated authorities.

- **Administrators Who Introduce a Discernment Process Must Be Willing to Commit Themselves to the Process**
  Regressing into an authoritarian mode after introducing a discernment process only invites disillusionment.

- **Discernment Is Just**
  Oppression is not the fruit of the Holy Spirit.

ship, the bishop's betrayal of his people's trust undermines his ability to be an effective Christian leader. Inconsistent behavior, especially by those who hold authority, is a detriment to discernment.

The chart on the previous page outlines some insights into discernment that might be gleaned from Case Two.

Case Three: Patricia and Jim

The Case

Pat and Jim are raising four children and realize more and more the blessings God has given to their family. In their prayer together, they feel called to give something back to those who are less fortunate. As a result they become involved with a local homeless shelter.

Once every two weeks, Pat volunteers to prepare and serve a meal at the local shelter. While she is gone, Jim takes responsibility for the children. This effort requires sacrifice of Jim, Pat and the children, but when the family prays, they feel that God is asking this sacrifice of them.

The shelter has few volunteers. Finances for the shelter are scarce and recent fundraising attempts have been amateur and unsuccessful. Pat has fundraising experience and influential connections. Before she realizes it, Pat finds herself organizing the annual fundraising campaign.

One evening as Pat is leaving the shelter, the director informs her that there is no one available to handle crisis calls coming into the shelter. The director asks if she and Jim would take the crisis calls at their home two evenings a week until another volunteer can be found. Knowing that the calls at times involve life-and-death situations, Pat cannot refuse.

Jim is angry when Pat informs him of the crisis calls. The phone rings often during the night. Jim and Pat are exhausted trying to respond to those less fortunate while nurturing their own children. Their relationship begins to show signs of strain.

One day, Pat is at the shelter working on fundraising and forgets to pick up her daughter, Molly, at three-o'clock from kindergarten. Coming home, Pat frantically makes six-o'clock dinner while Jim calls the children to the table. Molly's place is empty. Pat, realizing her mistake, rushes to Molly's school and finds her daughter frightened, cold and huddled underneath a bush on the school lawn.

Appalled at what they had done, Pat and Jim immediately withdraw from all involvement at the shelter. Initially they experience great relief. When concern for the poor becomes a focus of Pat and Jim's prayer, they easily correct their inclination to generosity by remembering their experience with the shelter. As the months go by, Pat and Jim do not experience the energy and joy that they had known in their initial work at the shelter. They interpret this emptiness as the price of recovering from their naive belief that they could make a difference in the world and raise a family at the same time.

Questions on Case Three

1. What role might consideration for the poor play in one's discernment processes?
2. What fruits are you noticing?
3. Are you comfortable with Pat and Jim's decision?

Analysis of Case Three

Pat and Jim are responsible parents who love their children and are grateful for all that God has given them. The spirit of prayer and gratitude in their lives is a fruit of the Holy Spirit. Their witness of prayer and sensitivity to the poor exemplifies a desire to live their Christian faith in the midst of daily life. Their married love is generative on many levels.

Pat and Jim's error is not generosity, but overextended generosity. Initially in prayer together, Pat and Jim discern to serve one meal every other week at the shelter.

Gradually additional duties are added to this initial decision. Pat and Jim take on these duties without carefully testing them in prayer and dialogue. In doing this, they violate their usual common sense. Eventually the additional good works overburden Pat and Jim's ability to be generous.

Accepting the added responsibilities of fundraising activities and crisis calls does not produce good fruits for Pat and Jim's family or for those at the shelter. The overextension of Pat and Jim's discernment brings harm to Molly, compromises Pat and Jim's relationship and erodes the family's commitment to the poor. In the end, overstated generosity leaves the poor isolated in their poverty, and leaves Jim and Pat's family empty in their giftedness. These are not fruits of the Holy Spirit.

Insights into Discernment from Case Three

- **Discernment Must Be Done Within the Context of One's Primary Relationships**
  Pat, Jim and the children need to prayerfully discern within the context of their family life.

- **One Must Be Clear About the Limits of What One Has Discerned**
  Overextensions of what one has discerned often do not bring good fruit.

- **The Holy Spirit May Call Us to Sacrifice, But Will Not Call Us into Frenzy**
  Frenzy that is disruptive to primary responsibilities needs to be carefully examined.

The Christian spiritual tradition has referred to this type of overstatement of good which brings unfortunate fruits as "an angel of darkness masquerading as an angel of light." The final chapter of this text will explore this topic more thoroughly.

Case Four: The "Three, Two, One, Method"

The Case

Churches hierarchically organized are not the only ones who have recently suffered from discernment disasters. Democratic churches also have stories to tell. One of the most delightful was related by a workshop participant.

At the beginning of a Christian leadership workshop, the participants were asked to formulate a definition of discernment from their own experiences of participating in discernment processes. During the sharing that followed, an elderly gentleman informed the assembly that his congregation used the "Three, Two, One, Method" of discernment. The facilitator asked him to explain. The gentleman informed the group that, when voting on issues, leaders of his congregation were asked not only to raise their hands voting "yes" or "no," but also to raise one, two or three fingers registering their attachment to their vote.

Later in the day, the facilitator asked the group to reflect upon the effectiveness of their congregational discernment processes using criteria she had presented. During the sharing that followed, the same gentlemen reflected that when voting on emotional issues, the "Three, Two, One, Method" tended to polarize his congregation. When this happened, points were simply added and the strongest side won. Politicking to win votes became an almost accepted procedure.

Questions on Case Four

1. Can politicking play a role in discernment processes?
2. What fruits of the "Three, Two, One, Method" caused the participant to question its true effectiveness?

Analysis of Case Four

Case Four tries to measure attachment in the discernment process. The elderly gentleman's congregation attended not only to their leaders' commitment to a particular issue, but also to their leaders' attachment to the issue. Although initially the "Three, Two, One, Method" seemed fair and responsive, upon reflection it was observed that it polarized the congregation and encouraged politicking. This kind of divisiveness is not a fruit of the Holy Spirit.

The Christian spiritual tradition suggests that persons approach discernment without attachment and even with indifference.[2] This indifference enables one to listen to the wisdom of the Holy Spirit without inordinate attachment and helps people move freely as the Spirit leads.

When one is attached to one's opinion, it is difficult to listen to other's viewpoints with openness. The Spirit cannot reveal when we are full of our own revelations.

The tradition also suggests that the Holy Spirit is not particularly fond of democratic voting processes. Monastic rules, for example, while encouraging familial dialogue, do not advocate democratic voting procedures. Rather, they suggest that the Lord has a fondness for speaking through those who are young and vulnerable.[3] If they desire to find the voice of the Holy Spirit, those who are leaders in the community must listen with openness to the young and the poor.

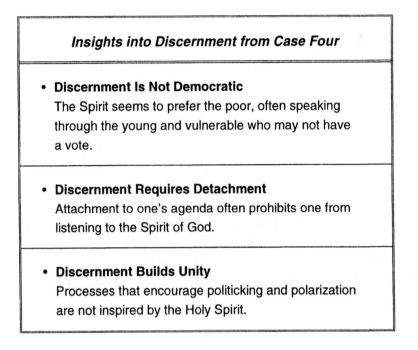

Insights into Discernment from Case Four

- **Discernment Is Not Democratic**
  The Spirit seems to prefer the poor, often speaking through the young and vulnerable who may not have a vote.

- **Discernment Requires Detachment**
  Attachment to one's agenda often prohibits one from listening to the Spirit of God.

- **Discernment Builds Unity**
  Processes that encourage politicking and polarization are not inspired by the Holy Spirit.

Common Sense, Scripture and Tradition

We have pondered contemporary cases through the lenses of common sense, scripture and tradition. Through this reflection we have formulated valuable insights into the mystery of discernment. Common sense, scripture and tradition are reputable guides.

Core to religious faith is the desire to live one's daily life according to the scriptures. Because every culture and era plays human challenges in a slightly different tonality, Christians throughout the ages have formulated responses to the scriptures. Tradition carries time-proven ways that Christians have learned to live the message of the scriptures in their own age. Because Christians continue to live the scriptures in the present age, tradition includes both the past and present. Christian tradition is a living tradition.[4]

While we may not be able to reason to Christian faith, Christian faith is reasonable. Christians of every age have reconciled truths from science and philosophy with their Christian faith. God's truth is revealed in the world. Using common sense as a measuring rod in one's search for God's presence in daily life is a thoroughly Christian concept. To claim that Christian wisdom cannot be reconciled with the material world is to fail in Christian orthodoxy.[5]

Discernment is a practical gift of the Holy Spirit illustrated in the scriptures and wrestled with by Christians of many ages and cultures. If we seek to use the language of discernment in our congregations and in our personal lives, we would do well to learn from the experiences of our brothers and sisters in faith. The following chapters explore stories, literature and cases from scripture, the spiritual tradition and contemporary life in which Christians continue to gain insight and to organize their insights concerning the mystery of discernment. To do this, Christians must continually distinguish between that in the world which will bring true life from that which is false.

Those searching the scriptures for models of discernment often note the prophets' ability to understand God's ways in the midst of the world. Some prophets are challenged to speak painful truths to people they deeply love; others are challenged to temper their insight by God's insistence that truth can be mediated only through love. Israel's task was to discern the prophets who spoke the Word of God from false prophets. The challenge of knowing how to discern cultural voices that are true to God's Word from those that are false is no less relevant today.

In the next chapter, the prophet Amos is studied as an introduction to the art of discerning the true from false prophets. Criteria used to discern true from false prophets are gathered from the Amos story and from samples of other prophetic literature. Additional scriptural models, i.e., Abraham, Moses, Jeremiah, Jonah, Jesus, Paul, the early Christian community, etc., could similarly be pondered.

Further Questions for Reflection/Discussion

1. If you could change aspects of the four discernment cases presented, what would you change and why?

2. In the cases presented, did the guides of common sense, scripture and tradition give you other insights into discernment?

3. Reflect on an experience of discernment from your own life. How might common sense, scripture and tradition guide your own case?

Suggestions for Further Reading

Barry, William A., S.J. *Paying Attention to God.* Notre Dame, IN: Ave Maria Press, 1990. Barry explores intimacy in prayer and resistances to intimacy with God. His book is helpful to those who are just beginning to learn to notice the movements of God in their everyday life.

Farley, Margaret A. *Personal Commitments: Beginning, Keeping, Changing.* San Francisco: Harper, 1986. Margaret Farley reflects upon the meaning of commitment, freedom and obligation in commitment, and commitment in light of the Jewish-Christian concept of covenant. The case studies she introduces invite the reader to think seriously not only about theories of commitment but also about the dynamics of commitment within the context of human relationships. Respect for personal commitments is essential to reflection regarding discernment.

Lewis, C.S. *The Great Divorce.* New York: Collier Books, 1946. In this delightful story, C.S. Lewis portrays a bus that stops in hell to pick up people to take them to heaven. The people that find themselves on this bus are not "bad" people, but each has a quirk, a gripe or an attachment that cripples their ability for true relationship. Although a fantasy, the book provides many cases for thought and discussion.

2

Discerning True
from False Prophets

❧ ❧

The Prophet Amos

Amos was an ordinary person. He worked as a herdsman.
God took Amos from following the flock and sent him as
a prophet to Israel (Am 7:14-15). At the time Israel was
enjoying prosperity and seemed blessed by God. This prosperity, however, had mixed consequences. Its cities became
crippled with immorality as the rich squandered resources
while the poor lacked necessities (Am 4:1). Although the
Israelites fulfilled the prescriptions of worship, their neglect of the poor betrayed the shallowness of their piety.

The Lord took Amos from his flocks and sent him to
the people as a prophet (Am 7:14-15). In his preaching,
Amos challenged Israel's perfunctory worship and insisted
that true love of God must be manifested in love of neighbor
(Am 5:21-24). Practical consequences follow behavior that
disavows the human rights of others. Amos warned Israel
that God could not continue to bless a nation whose economic and social systems tipped the balances to promote
luxury for some and poverty for others (Am 8:4-14). This
message set him at odds with both civil and religious leaders.

Religious authorities found Amos' message particularly
offensive (Am 7:10-12). Prosperity is good for keeping temples open. The temples were providing respectable and
needed services; perhaps they were even doing some social
outreach. Should the structures of civil and religious insti-

tutions change because of the opinions of someone who suddenly proclaims himself a prophet? Should not indiscriminate civil and cultic criticism be tempered so that law and order can be maintained? Can a prophet who presumes the right to comment not only on religious principles but also on socioeconomic structures truly be sent by God?

Since one's livelihood, values and socioeconomic status reflect one's position in established social structures, those who are favored often find criticism of existing structures offensive. Questioning the foundations of established structures can be perceived as threatening the very existence of a society. Institutions confer legitimate authority on those who pledge to preserve the foundations of a society. With the foundation in place, society can maintain its order and insure the quality of its life.

Amos questioned the foundations of his society because he could not reconcile human destitution and the love of God. Amos looked into the eyes of those who were impoverished in Israel. He realized something must be wrong with a system that did not recognize those in its midst who lacked basic human necessities.

Eventually Amos' vision and the need of the religious authorities to preserve basic structures collided. Amaziah, the priest of Bethel, appears before King Jeroboam and accuses Amos of conspiracy (Am 7:10-11). Amaziah then goes to Amos and advises him to flee from Israel into Judah (Am 7:12). If Amos stays in Israel, his message undermines the efforts and frustrates the intentions of legitimate civil and religious leadership. Controversy around Amos' message is escalating and tempers are wearing thin. In Judah, Amos will be further away from the institution and not so likely to cause trouble. A prophet is safer on the fringes.

Amos responds to Amaziah's well-intentioned advice by telling the priest that his wife will become a common prostitute and that his children will all die by the sword (Am 7:16-17). Prophets have the tendency to neglect niceties.

The prophetic tradition is filled with characters such as Amos who look at their world and accuse good people of not being faithful to love of God and love of neighbor. Prophets peer into socioeconomic situations and speak their secrets. They focus on the forgotten people in a society and insist on rendering them visible. They are a nuisance to the status quo.

Prophets are people whose deepening relationship with God invites them to see life from God's perspective. As they walk in daily relationship with God, they begin to see their neighbor with new eyes. People who are poor, who are hungry, who are lonely become visible to them. Prophets become distressed by the callous wastefulness of the rich and the poverty of the destitute. They begin to speak this distress.

Amos is demanding more from the rich than a benefactor's handout. He is telling civil and religious leadership that what is needed is a change in the structure of the social order. He insists that the rich share the rights to resources with the poor. He challenges the Israelites to bring their lives into conformity with the worship they perform.

Prophecy and Institutional Religion

In the days of Amos, many claimed to be prophets sent by God. In every age there are those who claim to have the salvific key to success and happiness. Followers gather and prophets who are popular one day are defamed the next. Observing this phenomenon, one may wonder if it is wise simply to remain aloof from prophetic types. It is best, perhaps, not to mix politics with religion.

Established religion is uncomfortable with the prophet who insists that love of God must be accompanied by a societal restructuring that concretely expresses love for one's neighbor, especially for the poor. It is easier to give handouts than to give up one's political-economic advantage. Amaziah, eager to maintain the status quo, sends Amos into exile (Am 7:10-13).

The prophet pays a high price. Amos is exiled by the very religious institution that originally nurtured his relationship with God.

On the other hand, institutional religion can provide society with a basic moral framework and with the organization of communal worship. When people are not invited into a context of moral discipline and regular prayer and worship, their lives can focus solely on competition and excess. Common moral practice and communal worship keep the conscience of a community alive.

Perhaps the prophet is wrong to challenge the institutions of religion. It is one thing to address the wrongs of society; it is another thing to challenge religious structures. Without religious institutions, society tends to degenerate into chaos. Prophets often alienate and frustrate good people. How, then, can one discern whether a prophetic voice has the potential of leading people towards a greater love of God and neighbor or of entangling people in an antisocial and destructive web?[1]

Criteria for Discerning True and False Prophets

There is perhaps nothing worse than the tyranny of the self-proclaimed prophet. The false prophet can play on people's good will, convince them to give of their lives and their resources, and then disappear without responsibility.

Even more dangerous is the one who puts on the airs of a prophet but then preaches only the good news people want to hear (Jer 6:13-14; Ezek 13:8-10). These prophets are often liked by political and religious institutions because they provide a mystic seal for the status quo. They serve to confirm people in social irresponsibility.

Clearly there is need for criteria by which those desiring God might distinguish the true from the false prophet.[2] The prophetic literature suggests some of these signs. Today in a world filled with many diverse voices, these biblical criteria find new relevance.

One sign that distinguishes the true from the false prophet is a conversion story in which *the true prophet speaks of a personal meeting with God* (Am 7:14-15; Ezek 1-3; Ex 3-4). It is within the context of religious experience that the true prophet receives the call to prophesy. The religious experience of the prophet is not planned or manipulated. It seems to happen in the midst of ordinary life and prayer.

For example, Isaiah has a vision of God's glory. Seeing himself before the glory of God, Isaiah understands that by himself he cannot speak God's word. He is a man of unclean lips. In response to Isaiah's realization of weakness, a seraph touches his mouth with a burning coal. After this purification, Isaiah can respond to the call of God. He is given words to speak which are in accord with the Word of God (Isa 6).

Early in his career, Jeremiah experienced the God-given command to prophesy in a way similar to Isaiah (Jer 1). Later, realizing that the fruits of prophecy were not always pleasant, Jeremiah complained to God about the burden of prophecy. Examining his heart, he realized that a burning fire had been placed within him. If he tried not to prophesy, the fire would ravage his being. To relieve his weariness he found himself shouting the prophecy of God (Jer 20:7-9).

Obviously a false prophet can fabricate a story relating a religious experience. Other signs are needed to distinguish the true from the false prophet.

A second sign is that *a true prophet proclaims a message that is contrary to the dominant mood.* This contrary message eventually proves itself true. If Israel enjoys peace and prosperity, true prophets proclaim doom and poverty. If Israel is suffering and exiled, the true prophet brings solace and encouragement. Ezekiel prophesies against false prophets who have proclaimed peace saying that God will visit their false peace with a deluge of rain and hailstones (Ezek 13:1-16). To a people tried by exile Isaiah offers a message of comfort (Isa 40:1-2).

Yet, a true prophet is not simply a contrary person. Prophets are judged to be authentic only if time proves their contrary words true (Deut 18:21-22; Ezek 33:33; Jer 28:9).

Third, *true prophets live as servants of Divine Authority.* Although at times a true prophet seems to be able to influence God (Exod 32:7-14; Am 7:1-3), true prophets act as divine messengers rather than on their own authority. At times the true prophet can be at odds with God concerning the prophetic mission. The prophet Jonah was faithful to his mission of proclaiming doom upon the sinful city of Nineveh (Jon 3:3-4). What he did not expect was that the people of Nineveh would repent (Jon 3:5-9). When God decided to show mercy because of Nineveh's contrition, Jonah became angry (Jon 4:1-4). In protest, Jonah challenged God's mercy and tried, through rather adolescent behavior, to manipulate God into displaying a bit of justifiable wrath. Jonah went out of the city, built a booth and waited for the fireworks (Jon 4:5). God, however, did not cooperate with Jonah's agenda (Jon 4:6-11). Jonah's inability to control God gives him credibility as a true prophet.

Lastly, *true prophets live moral lives.* They are not given to immorality, drunkenness or deceit (Jer 23:14-15; 29:21-23). They obey the bottom-line rules of society regarding the use of money, sex and recreational substances. The conduct of true prophets mirrors the integrity of the Word of God they claim to speak. If this integrity is lacking, the genuineness of the prophet is suspect (Jer 28:7).

One proof of the prophet's moral quality is the prophet's fidelity to Yahweh. Any prophet who encourages the people to follow other gods cannot be a true prophet (Deut 13:1-5; Jer 23:13). A prophet sent by God does not lead the people into apostasy.

Biblical Criteria for Discerning a True Prophet

- **A Personal Meeting with God**
  True prophets speak of a personal meeting with God in which they have a profound conversion experience.

- **A Contrary Message Which Proves Itself True**
  True prophets proclaim a message contrary to the dominant mood. This contrary message eventually proves itself true.

- **An Inability to Manipulate God**
  True prophets are servants of divine authority. As servants they are unable to manipulate God.

- **A Moral Lifestyle**
  True prophets live a moral life. They obey the bottom-line rules of society regarding the use of money, sex and recreational substances.

Limitations of Criteria for Discernment

Contemplating the above criteria, it is still possible to imagine being duped by a person who claims to bring God's message but in the end bears divisive and unloving fruits. Many false prophets lead exemplary lives, are convinced they have received a genuine call from God, speak words that are contrary to the social norm and claim to preach the word of God.

Thus, although the criteria for discernment provide general guidelines in discerning true from false prophets, they are not foolproof. Because discernment happens within the context of relationship, what is true to particular relationships sometimes can only be ascertained over time. Israel often discovered its genuine prophets only after a predicted disaster or blessing occurred. Sometimes hard truths are discovered after the facts.

The prophet may not have the most amiable personality, but the prophet is persistent about the truth seen. A prophet's contrariness is both gift and liability. The world needs those who challenge the status quo. A civil society requires voices that speak the perspective of those who are rendered invisible. The prophetic voice serves as the conscience of a society. Those who attempt to repress this conscience court disaster.

Society also needs to be discerning about its contrary people. Not every maverick should be followed. A prophet sees injustice but often fails to communicate this vision in a way that can be heard and sustained by a community. The gift of the prophet is the capacity to shock people out of their denial. The liability of the prophet is that their words are often experienced as threatening and unloving.

Often a community is capable of hearing the prophetic voice only after they have silenced it. A community needs to preserve some semblance of stability even in its conversion processes. While the gift of an established community is order and stability, the prophetic gift is justice and conversion. God's Spirit uses the gifts and limitations of the prophetic voice and also respects the wisdom of legitimate authority whose concern for social stability helps people feel safe while moving into new forms of consciousness.

The biblical criteria for discerning the true from the false prophet are guidelines that can be used in the daily struggle to love God and neighbor. There are no foolproof methods for discerning that which is true from that which is false. One reason for this is that no person or message is ever totally true or false. No person, not even the prophet, can discover the voice of the Spirit in isolation. A community made up of teachers, preachers, prophets, workers, leaders, children, etc., is needed to find the voice of the Holy Spirit who speaks within and among believers (1 Cor 12).

Discerning true and false prophets is a task that challenges Christian people in their daily living. True and false prophets live in one's outer world and one's inner world. The air is filled with many voices. One needs to choose. Sometimes, to hear at all, one needs silence. Contemporary people often attempt to listen to everything all the time. They fill themselves with so many outside voices that they gradually lose the ability to distinguish.

The inner world also has many voices. One's personality has a voice. One's personal history has a voice. One's moods, passions, inclinations and desires have a voice. All these voices need to be continually discerned. The purpose of silence is to give the heart and mind an opportunity to notice these voices that they might be distinguished.

Although the prophetic criteria for discernment can help sort the true from the false, these criteria cannot be applied simplistically. For example, using the fourth criterion, which deals with the moral life of a prophet who does not lead the people into apostasy, it would seem that any voice moving a person away from the worship of the one God could be judged false. Often, however, as one moves into a more loving relationship with God, one discovers that one's previous image of God is no longer adequate. Sometimes when this shift in imaging God occurs, people feel as if they are moving away from God. In reality they are growing into deeper relationship with God. The fourth criterion, while it objectively holds, could be misinterpreted by one who is in the throes of a shifting God-image.

One must also exercise some common sense regarding the first criterion that situates the prophetic call within the context of a religious experience. Many people have had experiences of God that have shaped the course of their lives. Ordinary people often dismiss these experiences thinking that a genuine experience of God is reserved for people whose caliber of holiness supposedly exceeds theirs.

These people have misinterpreted the criterion of religious experience. They have presumed that God's revelation occurs in ways that are beyond ordinary human experience. They have assumed that God speaks in celestial realms but is not interested in being with people in the midst of their daily lives. Their apparent humility in insisting that God cannot break through their unworthiness is in reality a blindness to the grace of God working in their lives.

On the other hand, religious experience is a gift. It cannot be forced. Those who try to manipulate themselves into a religious experience play God. They have an image of religious experience that they are trying to force upon God. Loving relationship cannot flow from this dynamic.

Using Criteria for Discerning a True Prophet

Case One: Is Jesus a True Prophet?

Religious people contemporary with Jesus struggled to discern the authenticity of Jesus' message. The following passage is a story of one town's grappling with the person of Jesus:

> He left that place and came to his hometown, and his disciples followed him. On the Sabbath he began to teach in the synagogue, and many who heard him were astounded. They said, "Where did this man get all this? What is this wisdom that has been given to him? What deeds of power are being done by his hands! Is not this the carpenter, the son of Mary and brother of James and Joses and Judas and Simon, and are not his sisters here with us?" And they took offense at him. Then Jesus said to them, "Prophets are not without honor, except in their hometown, and among their own kin, and in their own house." And he could do no deed of power there, except that he laid his hands on a few sick

people and cured them. And he was amazed at their
unbelief (Mk 6:2-6).

Questions for Reflection/Discussion

1. Using the criteria for discerning true prophets, would you
   identify Jesus as a true or false prophet?
2. What areas are you struggling with in your life that have
   to do with discerning what is true from what is false?

Other Scriptural Cases

Below are a number of passages from the New Testament:

Mt 7:15-23	2 Cor 11:1-15	Mt 12:22-37
Gal 5:1-25	1 Cor 2:6-16	1 Jn 4:1-6
1 Cor 14:26-33		

After reflecting on these passages, identify key elements of discernment in each text. Do these texts contribute
to the criteria for discerning a true prophet?

Summary

Prophets are people who strive to contemplate life from
God's perspective. Fidelity to prayer and personal experiences of God's love help the prophet realize that God can
indeed be trusted. Prophets speak what they sense is God's
Word even when it is contrary to the prevailing mood,
demands from them exemplary conduct and compels them
to speak and act in ways that often challenge established
civil and religious structures.

As the conscience of the community, the prophetic
character confronts injustice and demonstrations of religious piety that legitimate or ignore oppression. This con-
frontation frustrates those with lawful responsibility for
maintaining social order. While the prophet demands

restructuring, the institution requires stability. One must discern both the prophetic voice and the institutional voice.

Ordinary people are confronted daily with inner and outer voices. Some of these voices call them to conversion; others call them to stability and order. A loving relationship is a dance of change and stability.

The mystery of how one loves another is revealed as one struggles to love. Israel, trying to remain faithful in its love of God, learned skills for distinguishing the true prophetic voice from the false one. The Israelites realized that, in spite of their good intentions, they could be duped into beliefs and actions that were contrary to their desire to love. As the Hebrews struggled with the prophets in their midst and learned from experience, certain patterns emerged which helped them distinguish voices that were true and voices that were false.

Applying the principles of discernment within the context of a loving relationship reduces the risk of simplistic interpretation. This is true of any wisdom applied to personal relationships. Though a list of do's and don't's will not make a marriage, words of wisdom from those who have been married are often helpful to newlyweds. In the same way, criteria for discerning true prophets from false prophets will not automatically insure loving relationships with God and neighbor. The prophetic tradition does, however, offer the wisdom of experience to those who struggle to be faithful.

Suggestions for Further Reading

Brueggemann, Walter. *The Prophetic Imagination*. Philadelphia: Fortress Press, 1978. Brueggemann explores the vocation of a prophet to challenge the enculturation of religion, to evoke social consciousness, to imagine a new social order faithful to love of God and neighbor, and to inspire people to work towards a just and loving future.

McNamara, Martin. "Discernment Criteria in Israel: True and False Prophets." In *Discernment of the Spirit and of Spirits*, ed. Casiano Floristán and Christian Duquoc. Concilium: Religion in the Seventies Series. New York: The Seabury Press, 1979, pp. 3-13. This article is a brief survey of the prophetic tradition in the ancient world both within and outside of Israel. McNamara outlines criteria that Israel found helpful in distinguishing the true prophet from the false prophet.

Woodward, Evelyn. "Orientations." Chap. in *Poets, Prophets and Pragmatists*. Notre Dame, IN: Ave Maria Press, 1987, pp. 13-43. Although written as a guide for those involved in the renewal of religious life, the first chapter in Woodward's book takes seriously the gifts of the poets, prophets and pragmatists in a Christian community. Personal and communal reflection questions are offered at the end of the chapter to help readers reflect upon the gifts of the poets, prophets and pragmatists in their midst.

3

Discernment:
A Long Christian Tradition

Exploring Christian Literature

The Christian tradition is filled with accounts of good people who have struggled to be truthful and sensitive in their relationships with God, neighbor and creation. Christians in every age have been challenged to discern God's voice in the midst of daily life.[1]

This chapter explores excerpts from Christian literature which articulate the human struggle to discern God's spirit. Although no individual text synthesizes the fullness of the theme of discernment in the Christian tradition, each of the following selections offers insight as to how one might foster just and loving relationships with God, others and creation. It is hoped that by pondering these writings, the reader might better appreciate the multifaceted dimensions of the mystery of discernment in the Christian tradition.

Saint John of the Cross

The first excerpt is by a Spanish Carmelite, St. John of the Cross (1542-1591), and was most likely written in Segovia, Spain between 1588 and 1589. A certain nun who has the tendency to overstate the importance of her personal religious experiences is causing havoc within her monastery. Anyone who has been in a group afflicted with someone convinced that s/he is holier than the rest can be sympathetic with

31

this monastery's dilemma. John offers some practical advice for dealing with this sensitive issue.

> In the affective attitude this religious bears there appear to be five defects which reveal that hers is not a good spirit.
>
> First, it seems she has within her spirit a great attachment to possessing things, whereas the good spirit is always very detached in its appetites.
>
> Second, she is too secure in her spirit and has little fear of being inwardly mistaken. . . .
>
> Third, it seems she has the desire to persuade others that her experiences are good and manifold. A person with a genuine spirit does not desire to do this. . . .
>
> Fourth—and this is the main fault—the effects of humility do not appear in her attitude. When favors are genuine, as she says here that hers are, they are ordinarily never communicated to a soul without first undoing and annihilating it in the inner abasement of humility. And if these favors had produced this effect in her, she would not have failed to say something about it here, and even a great deal. For the first thing the soul esteems and is eager to speak of are the effects of humility. . . .
>
> Fifth, the style and language she uses doesn't seem to come from the spirit she claims, for the good spirit itself teaches a simpler style, one without the affectation or exaggeration she uses. And all this about what she said to God and God said to her seems to be nonsense.
>
> I would advise that they should not command or allow her to write anything about this, and that her confessor should not show willingness to hear of it, other than to hold it in little esteem and contradict it. Let them try her in the practice of sheer virtue, especially in self-contempt, humility, and obedi-

ence; and by the sould of the metal when tapped,
the quality of soul caused by so many favors will
show itself. And the trials must be good ones, for
there is no devil that will not suffer something for
his honor.[2]

Qualities of One Whose Spirit Is from God
St. John of the Cross

- **Detachment and Simplicity**
  A person who is in love with the Holy Spirit lives a life with
  little inner and outer clutter.

- **A Healthy Sense of Self-Doubt**
  Persons who do not absolutize their own judgments are
  more apt to listen to and learn from the wisdom of others.

- **Unpretentiousness**
  The modest person does not burden the community with
  bragging.

- **Strength Built on Weakness**
  God offers strength in weakness. Those who have suffered
  tend to be more empathic and effective in guiding others
  through similar dilemmas. When these people are
  complimented for their skills, they readily acknowledge that
  their strength flows out of their suffering.

- **Unaffectedness**
  Those who truly love God speak about that love in simple,
  straightforward language.

The response of John of the Cross is quite direct. He outlines the qualities of a person whose spirit is from God (see previous page).

Since the exaggeration this sister falls into is not helpful either to herself or to those she lives with, St. John suggests that she be tested by hardship to help her recognize the foolishness of her behavior. He also suggests that no one pay attention to the sister when she exhibits such behavior. This approach will perhaps help the woman realize that she is not as strong or as extraordinary as she thinks she is, and that she needs the wisdom and support of others.

Questions for Reflection/Discussion

1. What do you think about St. John's criteria for discernment? Can these criteria be used to discern the presence of the Holy Spirit today?

2. Is John a bit harsh in his evaluation and suggestions? Why or why not?

3. Can you think of experiences in your own life where you persisted in truth even when doing this made you appear unloving? How would you describe the relationship between truth and love?

C.S. Lewis

C.S. Lewis (1898-1963) was an English Christian writer. In his book *The Screwtape Letters*, Lewis imagines a master devil, Screwtape, writing to his nephew, an apprentice devil, Wormwood. Because the two devils are working against God, they refer to God as the "Enemy." Lewis' letters are delightful because he approaches Christianity from the underside. In so doing he says much about the daily struggle to live faithfully. Below is an excerpt from one of Screwtape's letters to Wormwood.

My dear Wormwood,

I am very pleased by what you tell me about this man's relations with his mother. But you must press your advantage. The Enemy will be working from the center outwards, gradually bringing more and more of the patient's conduct under the new standard, and may reach his behavior to the old lady at any moment. You want to get in first. Keep in close touch with our colleague Glubose who is in charge of the mother, and build up between you in that house a good settled habit of mutual annoyance: daily pinpricks. The following methods are useful.

1. Keep his mind on the inner life. He thinks his conversion is something inside him and his attention is therefore chiefly turned at present to the states of his own mind. . . . Encourage this. Keep his mind off the most elementary duties by directing it to the most advanced and spiritual ones. Aggravate that most useful human characteristic, the horror and neglect of the obvious. You must bring him to a condition in which he can practice self-examination for an hour without discovering any of those facts about himself which are perfectly clear to anyone who has ever lived in the same house with him or worked in the same office.

2. It is, no doubt, impossible to prevent his praying for his mother, but we have means of rendering the prayers innocuous. Make sure that they are always very "spiritual," that he is always concerned with the state of her soul and never with her rheumatism. . . .

3. When two humans have lived together for many years, it usually happens that each has tones of voice

and expressions of face which are almost unendurably irritating to the other. Work on that. . . .
4. In civilized life domestic hatred usually expresses itself by saying things which would appear quite harmless on paper (the *words* are not offensive) but in such a voice, or at such a moment, that they are not far short of a blow in the face. To keep this game up you and Glubose must see to it that each of these two fools has a sort of double standard. Your patient must demand that all his own utterances are to be taken at their face value and judged simply on the actual words, while the same time judging all his mother's utterances with the fullest and most oversensitive interpretation of the tone and the context and the suspected intention. She must be encouraged to do the same to him. Hence from every quarrel they can both go away convinced, or very nearly convinced, that they are quite innocent.

You know the kind of thing: "I simply ask her what time dinner will be and she flies into a temper. . . ."

Your affectionate uncle,
Screwtape [3]

Questions for Reflection/Discussion

1. What insights might be gained by looking at discernment from Screwtape's point of view?

2. Screwtape tends to concentrate his efforts on rather mundane events, moods and interactions. Why are these everyday events important to one's growth in relationship with God and neighbor?

The Life of Antony

St. Athanasius' book *The Life of Antony* is a classic in Christian spirituality. St. Athanasius wrote the work about a year after Antony's death in 357. Antony, an Egyptian, desirous of deepening his relationship with God, leaves the city and retreats into the desert. There he encounters many interior and exterior influences—some from God and some not from God. After nearly twenty years of prayer and asceticism, monks seeking guidance invade his desert solitude. The following is an exhortation Antony gives a group of these monks on the topic of discernment.

> For discrimination between the presence of the good and the evil is easy and possible, when God so grants it. A vision of the holy ones is not subject to disturbance, for he will not wrangle or cry aloud, nor will any one hear his voice. But it comes with such tranquility and gentleness that immediately joy and delight and courage enter the soul, for the Lord who is our joy, the power of God the Father, accompanies them. And the thoughts of the soul remain untroubled and calm so that shining brightly, it sees those who appear by its own light. The soul is overcome by a desire for divine and future realities, and it desires to be entirely united with these beings, if only it could depart in their company. But if some, being human, are frightened by the vision of the good spirits, those who appear remove their fear by means of love, as Gabriel did for Zacharias, and the angel who appeared in the holy sepulchre did for the women, and as did the one who said to the shepherds in the Gospel, fear not.
>
> The assault and appearance of the evil ones, on the other hand, is something troubling, with crashing and noise and shouting—the sort of disturbance one might expect from tough youths and robbers. From this come immediately terror of soul, confusion and

disorder of thoughts, dejection, . . . listlessness, grief
and fear of death; and finally there is craving for
evil, contempt for virtue, and instability of character. When, therefore, you are frightened on seeing
someone, if the fear is instantly removed, and its
place is taken by unspeakable joy and cheerfulness
and confidence and renewed strength, and calm-
ness of thought, and by the other things I mentioned
before, both bravery and love of God, be of good
courage and say your prayers. For the joy and the
stability of the soul attest to the holiness of the one
who is in your presence. So when Abraham saw the
Lord he rejoiced, and John jumped for joy at the
voice of Mary the God-bearer. But if, when certain
ones appear, a disturbance occurs and noise from
outside, and an apparition of a worldly kind, and
threat of death, and things I spoke of before, know
that the visit is from the wicked.

And let this too be a sign to you: When the soul
remains in fear, that is due to the presence of the
enemies. For the demons do not remove the fear
caused by such appearances, as the great Archangel
Gabriel did for Mary and for Zacharias, and the angel
who appeared at the tomb did for the women. On
the contrary, when they see people who are fearful,
they multiply the apparitions so as to terrify them
all the more, and then descend in order to malign
them. . . . But the Lord did not allow us to be
beguiled by the devil, and censuring him whenever
he made such appearances, he said, "Begone, Satan!" . . . Therefore let the crafty one be despised
by us more and more. . . .[4]

Antony, who was known for his gift of discernment,
learned to distinguish the presence of good and evil in his
life. He noticed that evil leaves a person in distress and
sadness. Good inclines a person toward joy and peace. One

distinguishes between the presence of good and of evil by observing the fruits produced.

For Christians good and evil are not equal opposites. Since Christ has conquered death, good has already triumphed over evil. Because God's love has overcome all evil, Christians can call upon this love when praying for those who injure them.

The following chart outlines Antony's comparison of the fruits of a good presence and the fruits of an evil presence. The fruits of good are placed in larger letters to remind readers that the comparison between good and evil is not a comparison of equals.

Discerning the Presence of Good and Evil The Life of Antony	
Presence of God	**Presence of Evil**
1. Is tranquil and gentle	1. Brings crashing, noise and shouting
2. Brings joy, delight and courage	2. Brings dejection, listlessness and grief
3. Produces untroubled and calm thoughts	3. Produces confused, disordered and troubled thoughts
4. Desires divine and future realities	4. Craves evil, has a contempt for virtue and encourages an unstable character
5. Removes fear by means of love	5. Brings fear and terror of soul

Questions for Reflection/Discussion

1. What insights regarding discernment does Antony's instruction offer you?

2. One of the gifts of the Holy Spirit is the fear of the Lord, and yet Athanasius suggests that fear does not come from God. How might one reconcile this apparent contradiction?

Saints Clare and Francis of Assisi

Two of the most popular Italian saints in Christian spirituality are Saints Clare (ca.1193-1253) and Francis of Assisi (1182-1226). Francis was the son of a wealthy merchant and Clare the daughter of a wealthy knight. Both decided to give up their economic privilege to follow more closely the poor, crucified Christ.

Francis and Clare founded new ways of living in religious community that remain to this day. Being a founder is no easy task. All their lives, Clare and Francis struggled to discern how they might continue to be faithful to the God they loved.

In the following story from the *Little Flowers*, Saint Francis is trying to decide whether to spend his life in prayer and solitude or to do occasional preaching. To come to a decision, he finds friends who know and love him. He asks them to pray about the matter that they might advise him.

> Saint Francis at the beginning of his conversion, when he had already gathered many companions and received them in the Order, was placed in a great agony of doubt as to what he should do: whether to give himself only to continual prayer or to preach sometimes. He wanted very much to know which of these would please Our Lord Jesus Christ most. And as the holy humility that was in him did not allow him to trust in himself or in his own prayers, he humbly turned to others in order to know God's will in this matter.
>
> So he called Brother Masseo and said to him: "Dear Brother, go to Sister Clare and tell her on my behalf to pray devoutly to God with one of her more spiritual companions, that God may deign to show me what is best: either that I preach sometimes or that I devote myself only to prayer. And then go also to Brother Silvester, who is staying on Mount Subasio, and tell him the same thing."

Brother Masseo went, and as St. Francis had ordered him, gave the message first to St. Clare and then to Brother Silvester. When the latter received it, he immediately set himself to praying. And while praying he quickly had God's answer. And went out at once to Brother Masseo and said: "The Lord says you are to tell Brother Francis this: that God has not called him to this state only on his own account, but that he may reap a harvest of souls and that many may be saved through him."

After this Brother Masseo went back to St. Clare to know what she had received from God. And she answered that both she and her companion had had the very same answer from God as Brother Silvester.

Brother Masseo therefore returned to St. Francis. And the Saint received him with great charity: he washed his feet and prepared a meal for him. And after he had eaten, St. Francis called Brother Masseo into the woods. And there he knelt down before Brother Masseo, and baring his head and crossing his arms, St. Francis asked him: "What does my Lord Jesus Christ order me to do?"

Brother Masseo replied that Christ had answered both Brother Silvester and Sister Clare and her companion and revealed that "He wants you to go about the world preaching, because God did not call you for yourself alone but also for the salvation of others."

And then the hand of the Lord came over St. Francis. As soon as he heard this answer and thereby knew the will of Christ, he got to his feet, all aflame with divine power, and said to Brother Masseo with great fervor: "So let's go—in the name of the Lord."

And he took as companions Brother Masseo and Brother Angelo, holy men. And he set out like a bolt of lightning in his spiritual ardor, not paying any attention to the road or path.[5]

One would certainly not bother one's friends with this type of discernment process on a regular basis! Three elements seem key to this discernment story. First, Francis is making a decision that is significant not only to him, but also to the brothers and sisters with whom he is committed to in community. A change in the direction of Francis' life will affect the lives of Clare and Silvester. Therefore, including these companions in his discernment process is an appropriate and loving action. Second, Francis carefully selects the friends he asks to advise him in this matter. He chooses friends who know the true desires of his heart and whom he trusts will discern within the context of prayer. Third, Francis takes Clare and Silvester's recommendation very seriously and acts immediately on the advice given him.[6]

Discernment Principles of St. Francis

- **Discern That Which Affects Others with Others**
  Discernment processes affecting significant others
  must include these others.

- **Discern with Mature People**
  Discernment requires spiritual and emotional maturity.
  When discerning, do not burden those who do not
  have sufficient maturity.

- **When the Spirit's Direction is Clear, Follow Immediately**
  One discerns to obediently follow the Holy Spirit.
  One loves the Holy Spirit when one offers a generous
  response.

Questions for Reflection/Discussion

1. Friends can help us find direction in our daily lives. What do you think about the method St. Francis used to involve his friends in his discernment process? Can you imagine yourself asking prayers and advice from your friends as Francis did from his?

2. Francis carefully chose friends to help him come to his decision. What characteristics would you look for in friends you might include in a discernment of this kind?

3. Can you think of times when asking for a friend's input into a decision might not be the best way to deal with a personal dilemma?

Teresa

The struggle to choose God's way is more difficult when one is confronted with violence, terror and personal tragedy. In the early 1980's, the Salvadoran government began brutal attacks against those who protested governmental injustice. Thousands of people were forced to leave the country, to go underground, or to engage in guerilla activity. This account is written in September, 1981 by a woman named Teresa who joined the guerrillas working as a nurse.

> When I was still living in San Salvador, I was once detained by two men from the security forces. They forced me at gunpoint to go with them to a vacant lot. They threatened to kill me. I could not escape. I cried and prayed, but they just taunted me. They threw me down on the ground and raped me until I fainted. After I regained consciousness, I was sick for eight days.
>
> Later, when I told my *compañeros* what had happened, they told me that the hatred I felt for my assailants would give me strength for my work. But I disagreed. I will always remember their faces, but I cannot hate them.

After that, I decided to come here to the mountains to work as a nurse. At first when there was combat, I was very frightened. I prayed to God asking for courage. Then I felt more confident that God would help me to continue my work here, taking care of the sick and wounded.

. . . [O]nce in the midst of a bombing, a woman began to give birth. . . . I tried to help the woman reach the bomb shelter, but she couldn't make it. We moved under a tree. The baby was born there as the bombs exploded around us. I was half-dead with fear. My legs wanted to run to the bomb shelter, but how could I leave the woman? The attack lasted an hour. We couldn't even cover the baby. There was dust in the air from the bombs, and the baby was in danger of getting tetanus. But, thanks to God, the mother and baby survived. . . .

Although we are fighting a war, we are not doing so because of hatred. We are motivated not by hatred but by a desire for a better world. God willing, this war will end.[7]

When life is pushed to its limits, when evil becomes nearly unbearable, there is basically only one decision to make. One either chooses love or hate. Teresa's choice is clear. Daily in her work and in her relationships she chooses love. She makes the choice for love because she desires a better world. In one sense there is very little to say about Teresa's choice. In another sense the radical choice to love in the midst of hate is the hardest and the most profoundly Christian of all choices.

Questions for Reflection/Discussion

1. Can it ever be God's desire that Christians choose to resist legitimate civil or church authority? If so, what criteria would need to be used to come to this decision?

2. What do you think allows Teresa to continue to do her work with love while living with the memory of her rape?

3. What does Teresa's desire for a better world have to do with discernment?

Summary

As seen from the above examples, the Christian spiritual tradition offers insight into the process of growing in loving relationship with God and others. The practical advice of John of the Cross, the discernment between the presence of GOOD and evil in the *Life of Antony,* the devious plots of Screwtape and Wormwood, the discernment of God's will in the story of Francis, Clare and Silvester, and Teresa's choice for love, all shed light on the multifaceted dimensions of discernment.

The Christian tradition is rich with the lives and writings of those who struggle to find God's spirit as they live and work with others and with all of creation. As individual threads, these pieces of wisdom need the hand of an artist to weave them into a tapestry highlighting both their individual contributions and their interconnectedness.

St. Ignatius of Loyola creates such a classic tapestry in his *Rules for Discernment*.[8] The remaining chapters of this book examine Ignatius' *Rules,* not as the first or only synthesis of the Christian tradition of discernment, but as a classic paradigm able to guide Christians who seek the Spirit of love in their daily lives.

Suggestions for Further Reading

Guillet, Jacques, Gustave Bardy, Francois Vandenbrouchke, Joseph Pegon and Henri Martin. *Discernment of Spirits.* Translated by Sister Innocentia Richards. Collegeville, MN:

The Liturgical Press, 1970. A survey of Christian writings beginning with scriptural sources and ending with pre-contemporary spiritual writers. The book is still one of the finest historical surveys on the theme of discernment in the Christian tradition.

Lienhard, Joseph T. "On 'Discernment of Spirits' in the Early Church," *Theological Studies* 41 (Sept. 1980): 505-29. Lienhard's work is a very helpful commentary on "Discernment of Spirits" in early Christian literature. Readers may find his commentary on discernment in Athanasius' *Life of Antony* on pages 514-517 of this article particularly beneficial.

Mueller, Joan. "The Theology of Discernment: A New Historical Overview," *Studies in Formative Spirituality* 12 (Feb. 1991): 105-118. This study surveys the theme of discernment in the history of Christian spirituality including some contemporary examples.

4

The Path of St. Ignatius

The Context of the *Rules*

To understand Saint Ignatius' *Rules for Discernment*, it is helpful to situate these *Rules* within the context of Ignatius' own life.[1] For Ignatius, the *Rules for Discernment* are not mere theoretical understandings of the spiritual life. They are, rather, a reflection upon his personal struggle.

Ignatius describes this struggle in his *Autobiography* that he writes at the insistence of his friends Father Nadal and Father Luis Gonzalez de Camara. Many men are joining the Society of Jesus, the religious order that Ignatius founded. Fathers Nadal and Luis Gonzalez de Camara feel that an autobiographical account of Ignatius' early inspiration would be helpful to those joining the order.

After much prompting, Ignatius recounts his story to Camara. His *Autobiography* recalls events between the years 1521-1538. Ignatius writes the *Rules for Discernment* at the beginning of this period. The *Autobiography* contextualizes the *Rules* within the framework of Ignatius' early life.

Noticing Inner Movements

The story begins in 1521. The French are attacking the fortress at Pamplona. Though clearly the Spanish can no longer offer resistance, Ignatius is doing all he can to persuade his commander to continue the battle.

After the assault has been in progress for some time, a cannonball shatters one of Ignatius' legs and seriously wounds the other. With Ignatius' fall, the Spanish surrender to the French. The French treat Ignatius kindly, and after a couple of weeks take the severely wounded man home to his family's castle in Loyola.

At first it seems doubtful that Ignatius will live, but eventually he begins his long convalescence. When he is well enough to feel the boredom of the long hours in bed, Ignatius asks for a book to read. He prefers romantic fiction, but this type of book is not available. Instead he is given the *Life of Christ* by Ludoph of Saxony and the *Golden Legend*, a book about the lives of the saints, by Jacobus de Voragine.

Ignatius reads and finds himself dreaming of following Christ like Saints Francis and Dominic. At other times he dreams of being in the service of a great lady.

> Nevertheless Our Lord assisted him, by causing these thoughts to be followed by others which arose from the things he read. For in reading the life of Our Lord and of the saints, he stopped to think, reasoning within himself, "What if I should do what St. Francis did, and what St. Dominic did?" Thus he pondered over many things that he found good, always proposing to himself what was difficult and burdensome; and as he so proposed, it seemed easy for him to accomplish it. But he did no more than argue within himself, saying, "St. Dominic did this, therefore I have to do it; St. Francis did this, therefore I have to do it." These thoughts also lasted a good while; then, other things coming in between, the worldly ones mentioned above returned, and he also stayed long with them. This succession of such diverse thoughts lasted for quite some time, and he always dwelt at length on the thought that turned up, either of the worldly exploits he wished to perform or of these others of God that came to

his imagination, until he tired of it and put it aside and turned to other matters.

Yet there was this difference. When he was thinking of those things of the world he took much delight in them, but afterwards, when he was tired and put them aside, he found himself dry and dissatisfied. But when he thought of going to Jerusalem barefoot, and of eating nothing but plain vegetables and of practicing all the other rigors that he saw in the saints, not only was he consoled when he had these thoughts, but even after putting them aside he remained satisfied and joyful.[2]

Those who are occupied with many things often pay little attention to their daydreams. Ignatius, however, discovers that reflecting upon his dreams adds color to his long, lonely convalescence. Ignatius studies his daydreaming by observing the moods and movements in his heart and mind. Gradually he learns how to distinguish those inner movements that prompt him toward greater love and those that leave him cold and desolate.

After Ignatius recovers, he spends a year in prayer and solitude in Manresa and then departs on pilgrimage to Jerusalem. Arriving in Jerusalem, he tries to associate himself with the Franciscans living there. Because of political upset in Jerusalem at the time, the Franciscans do not accept Ignatius' request and order Ignatius under the pain of excommunication to return home. Since it is obviously not God's will that he stay, Ignatius returns to Spain.

The Society of Jesus

Using what he learned about discernment over the course of his recuperation and pilgrimage, Ignatius continues to do spiritual direction. Realizing the need for formal education, he begins a course of studies. He eventually completes his studies in Paris where the first companions of the Society of Jesus join him.

Ignatius' hope is to go back to Jerusalem to work for the conversion of the Turks. He never fulfills this desire. Instead he spends the rest of his days administrating the rapidly growing Society of Jesus.

The *Rules* for Discernment

While he was recuperating, Ignatius discovered that some moods, inclinations, passions, desires, dreams, thoughts, etc., inclined him toward becoming a peaceful person, and some left him dry and restless. He learned to distinguish between that which moved him toward true relationship with God and others, and that which undermined these relationships.

Ignatius systematized his own experience of distinguishing movements to help others who were struggling to notice their own movements. His *Rules for Discernment* are the outline he used to guide himself and others in this task.

The Language of the Rules

Ignatius is a sixteenth century medieval man and his writing bespeaks his culture. If one wishes to explore the wisdom of another age and culture, one must sometimes excuse its ignorance even as one searches for its wisdom. This excusing, however, must be done with discretion. Biases that promote sexism, classism and/or racism must be distinguished from that wisdom that can be helpful to human persons of every culture, race and era. In the present case, the modern reader must distinguish Ignatius' offensive sexist stereotypes from his genius for observing and understanding human dynamics. In addition, moderns might find it helpful to understand Ignatius' militaristic language in terms of strategy and choice rather than in terms of warfare.

In the medieval world, outer reality, psychic reality and the spirit world were considered relevant. In contemporary life, the scientific world often glorifies empiricism and the psychological sciences at times give the impression that therapy is salvation. Many mainline Christians try to compress the world of the spirits into the world of the psyche.

Ignatius' brilliance is his consideration of the interrelationships between the empirical, psychological and spiritual. By contemplating the outer world, the inner world, and the world of the spirits, he illustrates why a person might wish to be discerning. One discerns to foster true and loving relationship with God, others and the world. Anything that inclines one away from this relationship cannot be from a "good spirit." Thus an "evil spirit" might be another's gossip against one that undermines relationship, a psychological maladjustment that prevents growth, or a malevolent spirit. In any case, the Christian's tactics are the same. One cooperates with a Good Spirit who moves one toward love of God, neighbor and the world; one works against an evil spirit that destroys these relationships.[3]

The *Rules* are divided into two sets. The first set of *Rules* is to be used in cases in which the presence of evil, sadness or confusion is evident. The second set is used in cases in which evil disguises itself as good.

While Ignatius does recognize the presence of the spirit world, the *Rules for Discernment* are not concerned with obsession or possession by evil spirits. Neither is Ignatius tempted to provide Christians with norms of judgment by which they might label other people as "good" or "evil." Ignatius' *Rules* are merely guides by which Christians might discern whether the inner and outer movements that are a part of their lives are moving them toward greater love of God, neighbor and the world or are edging them toward isolation and apathy.

The Purpose of the Rules

In his text, Ignatius outlines the purpose of the *Rules for Discernment:*

> Rules to aid us toward perceiving and then understanding, at least to some extent, the various motions which are caused in the soul: the good motions that they may be received, and the bad that they may be rejected.[4]

The purpose of the *Rules* is a simple one. The *Rules* exist to help people (1) **perceive** in order that they might (2) **understand** so that they might (3) **take appropriate action**—receiving the good motions and rejecting the bad. One might outline Ignatius' purpose as follows:

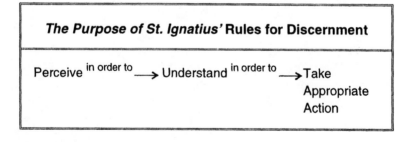

Perceiving

To discern, people must first notice the content of discernment—the diverse inner and outer movements of their daily lives. Those who do not notice outer movements fail to appreciate both the limitations and possibilities of their humanity. A person cannot discern without noticing the people, places and events that impact one's daily life.

Ignatius learned that he also needed to notice his inner movements before he could distinguish them. Inner movements include one's thoughts, feelings, passions, moods, tendencies, inclinations, desires, etc. Ignatius suggests that persons take time at noon and in the evening to examine themselves to become more attentive to these thoughts, feelings and responses.[5]

Although it is difficult to reconcile time for such self-examination with a hectic schedule, many people who take this time eventually discover that a reflective life is also an efficient life. Because reflection helps them get in touch with inner and outer movements and understand these movements, it is easier to discover appropriate courses of action. Persons who notice their inner and outer movements are more in touch with themselves and are often better able to relate with others.

Understanding

Human persons perceive with their senses. A man sees a building in the distance and says, "There's a store in the distance." A woman walks into her home, notices a wonderful aroma, and exclaims, "We're having chili for supper!" One's senses alert one that something is happening.

People associate particular sense responses with understandings they have acquired through life experience. The man surmises that the square frame in the distance is a store, because he has seen similar square frames that were indeed stores. The woman thinks she smells chili because she judges the aroma in the air to resemble the smell of chili she has enjoyed on previous occasions.

Data can be miscategorized. One can misunderstand. The man might think he sees a store, but in reality sees an abandoned barn. The woman might believe she is smelling chili, but is really smelling pizza.

The outer world can correct misunderstandings. The man comes upon the "store" hoping to find a telephone and instead finds that he has misidentified what truly is a barn. All the wishing in the world will not immediately make the barn into a store. The reality of the barn corrects his misconception. A mother comes home from work and can almost taste the chili that is for supper when her three-year-old daughter informs her that dad is making pizza. Although the woman may be disappointed, the evidence proves her judgment wrong. Indeed, pizza is being served.

Understanding that is inaccurate can lead to unintended or misinformed action. Decisions based on misunderstandings can exact a high price. The process of discernment, while concerned with action that promotes loving relationship, is also concerned about clear understanding. Healthy relationships with God, self, others and creation must be both true and loving.

Noticing without understanding overloads one with a hodgepodge of data that opens many possibilities for action but does not focus these varied possibilities. Understanding categorizes inner and outer data. This categorization of data clarifies possibilities for action.

Taking Appropriate Action

Information that a person has experienced through one's senses and categorized in one's mind invites appropriate action. If a woman identifies that chili is on the supper menu, she might refrain from snacking if she enjoys chili or make a sandwich if she does not. If a man is lost in a cornfield and believes that the object in the distance is a store, he may adjust his direction and move toward the store. If he is a fugitive, the identification of a store may encourage movement in the opposite direction. The course of life is influenced by what one experiences and how one identifies and interprets experience.

As noticing outer realities such as identifying a store or the aroma of chili prompts action, so noticing inner movements is also helpful in determining action. Ignatius suggests that people try to perceive and understand their desires, inclinations, tendencies, thoughts, feelings and passions to accept the direction of those that lead toward true and loving relationships and reject those that turn one away from these relationships.

These motions are understood "to some extent." The struggle to know oneself takes a lifetime. Learning to notice and identify the movements of one's heart is not a simple task. At times it can even be risky.

People who are unhappy in their work situations, for example, but do not reflect upon this unhappiness will never creatively face their frustration in a way that invites imaginative and productive alternatives. However, suppose these people notice their frustration and attempt to create alternatives, but find that management is not interested in recognizing employees' creative talents. Noticing and understanding without the possibility of action often intensifies frustration and jeopardizes seemingly stable relationships. Those who notice their inner passions, thoughts, feelings, inclinations, moods and desires may find themselves confronted with difficult choices. Sometimes it seems less challenging to proceed blindly.

Yet, an unreflective life is also costly. Not noticing inner and outer movements tends to fill one with gnawing dissatisfaction and despondent hopelessness. Dissatisfaction and hopelessness can slowly erode a person's emotional and moral character. People who harbor repressed irritation and anger often project this frustration onto those they love.

Practicing the Art of Reflection

In the following case study, readers are asked to explore the quality of Tom's noticing in order to examine their own perspectives concerning self-reflection. The case is divided into two scenarios. In the first, Tom has not acquired the art of reflection. In the second, Tom is becoming more aware of the inner and outer movements that affect his life.

Case One: Tom

Tom is a twenty-five year old man who is currently finishing a graduate program in engineering at a Christian university. He has a loving family and some good friends. He is generally liked by his professors.

Although Tom's life appears stable, Tom is having a hard time. His relationships with his classmates are often perceived by them as being excessively competitive. Tom tends to judge others quite severely and looks at life in general as a series of blacks and whites. He is a chain smoker.

Tom goes to a campus minister and describes his feelings of being up one day and down another. He tells the minister that he does not like the way he treats others sometimes, but that he really does not intend to be judgmental. His judgmentalism "just sort of happens." The minister asks Tom some questions about his family history, but Tom does not want to talk about his family.

After having a better week, Tom comes to the conclusion that he is being harassed by an evil spirit. He thinks he will feel better about himself if he attends more religious services and tries not to judge people anymore.

Questions for Reflection/Discussion

1. Is Tom perceiving and understanding what might be happening to him? What has he noticed? What hasn't he noticed?

2. What do you think about Tom's conclusion?

3. Can you identify with Tom's frustration over trying to be a good Christian person but struggling with some recurring faults? If you were Tom, what course of action would you choose?

Case Two: Tom—Ten Months Later

Introduction

Because Tom does not adequately notice the inner and outer movements affecting him, he cannot understand himself and does not know what to do when his moods get out of hand. If Tom would begin to notice these movements, he could probably sort which desires, inclinations, moods and tendencies move him toward true and loving relationships and which do not.

Below is a case study of Tom ten months later. Notice that Tom's life is not perfect, but that he has made significant progress. His progress can be attributed to his attempt to (1) **perceive** the inner and outer movements affecting his life in order to (2) **understand** them so that he might (3) **take appropriate action.**

The Case

It was not long before Tom discovered that ignoring inner and outer movements was not a helpful way to deal with his problems. After attending religious services three times a week and trying to work harder on his judgmentalism, Tom found himself more judgmental than ever.

One night Tom was studying for an exam and was very stressed. His lifelong friend Gerry came over to talk and Tom became very angry. Gerry challenged Tom regarding his excessive smoking and his vicious attitude.

After finishing his exam, Tom had time to think about the night before. Realizing he needed to do something about his temper, and feeling badly about hurting his friend, Tom began therapy. He also went back to the campus minister and asked for regular spiritual direction. The campus minister suggested that Tom take time each day for prayer and self-reflection.

In therapy, Tom gradually admitted that he was an adult child of an alcoholic father. Tom was able to identify some of the roots of his anger and, under the guidance of the therapist, began to change some of his patterns of behavior.

After a few months, Tom realized that he was not enjoying engineering school. He understood that his father had always wanted to be an engineer and realized that he had unreflectively taken on his father's dreams without considering his own. Tom knows now that he has some important decisions to make—decisions he is again tempted to avoid.

Questions for Reflection/Discussion

1. Has noticing inner and outer movements been helpful to Tom or has it only made him more miserable?

2. Is there a place for professional support in one's personal and spiritual life? When is this help appropriate? Might there be times when professional support would not be helpful?[6]

3. Can you identify with Tom's experience? If you were Tom, what would you find helpful? What might Gerry do to be supportive of Tom right now?

4. How might the Ignatian guide of perceiving and understanding so that one might act be helpful to Tom?

Summary

The *Rules for Discernment* help one focus life's movements toward true and loving relationships. That which is not good is not studied or analyzed, it is simply rejected. The Ignatian *Rules* teach one how to go about daily life calmly, diligently, intelligently and with a sense of humor.

The chapters that follow explore further St. Ignatius' *Rules for Discernment*. With each chapter the reader is invited to keep in mind that the purpose of these *Rules* is to help one:

Perceive ^{in order to} ——▶Understand ^{in order to} ——▶Take
Appropriate
Action

Suggestions for Further Reading

Dunne, Tad. "The Praxis of Noticing." In *Spiritual Mentoring.* San Francisco: Harper, 1991. Dunne develops six fundamental principles of noticing, discusses what one might notice, and moves into noticing consolation and desolation. His chapter expands what is presented in this text.

Ignatius of Loyola. "The Autobiography." In *Ignatius of Loyola: Spiritual Exercises and Selected Works,* ed. George E. Ganss, S.J., 65-111. New York: Paulist Press, 1991. Those who wish to study more fully how St. Ignatius learned the dynamics of discernment within the context of his life will want to read Ignatius' full "Autobiography."

5

Different Types of Persons

❧ ❦

Forming Christian Community

Good people gathered in one place for a specific purpose do not necessarily constitute a community. Even Christian people who have a mission, a common faith, and who wish to form community with each other often fail in their efforts.

One searches for the Holy Spirit in concrete historical circumstances. These circumstances include the people one associates with and to whom one is committed in relationship. One listens to the voice of God within the context of these relationships. One also tests what one believes to be the voice of God within these relationships.

Sometimes the complexity of human relationships leads one to question whether the voice of God can really be found among and between people. Our Christian faith says that it can. Yet, interpersonal dynamics within Christian communities are often characterized by self-righteous attitudes, gossip, denial, negativity and frustration. How, then, might one discover the Spirit of God who is claimed to be among and between believers?

Christian community is made up of individual persons who have their own personalities, biochemical makeups, gifts and liabilities. No human person is totally good or totally bad. One's gifts and liabilities are usually simply opposite sides of the same coin. If one is persevering, one is probably also stubborn. If one is a talented activist, one may have the tendency to run over people. Some might admire the organizational abilities of a person, while others will experience that same person as cold and aloof. If some are thought to be compassionate, others find their lack of organizational ability frustrating. With this as the human experience one can be amazed whenever an experience of Christian community occurs.

Even those the church has declared saints had their share of interpersonal difficulties. There is a saying in monastic circles that jests that it is very difficult for the ordinary monk to live with the saint. Saints tend to live on the edge of a truth. They are often canonized specifically to illuminate a specific truth. Those who live with them every day can grow a bit tired of this gift. The monastic saying jokes that those who live with saints, become saints.

Christian people struggle to form communities that are faithful to the movement of the Holy Spirit between and among themselves. In doing this they are required to listen to each others' hearts and to appreciate the diversity of both gifts and liabilities.

Communities need to be vigilant in listening to each member without allowing manipulation from the strong or tyranny from the weak. To do this, communities require an effective and charitable means of recognizing and relating to human strength and weakness. Ignatius' first two *Rules for Discernment* offer guidance for noticing the dynamics of good and evil when people are working out of their strengths (Rule 1:2) and when they are working from their weaknesses (Rule 1:1).

Working Out of Strength and Weakness

ॐ *Rule 1:1 Know Your Weakness* ॐ

Every personality has both strengths and weaknesses. St. Ignatius begins his *Rules for Discernment* by describing persons who are caught in their weakness. Rule 1:1 describes such persons.

Rule 1:1

> In the case of persons who are going from one mortal sin[1] to another, the enemy ordinarily proposes to them apparent pleasures. He makes them imagine delights and pleasures of the senses, in order to hold them fast and plunge them deeper in their sins and vices.
>
> But with persons of this type the good spirit uses a contrary procedure. Through their habitual sound judgement on problems of morality he stings their consciences with remorse.[2]

Ignatius carefully describes the work of evil. An evil spirit encourages a person who is caught in his/her weakness and does everything it can to act as a catalyst in this process. It does this not by encouraging the person to be bad, but by proposing "apparent pleasures."

Ignatius is not saying that pleasure is evil. What he is saying is that the choice of *false* pleasures can lead one away from relationship. An evil spirit helps persons imagine false pleasures and in this way lures them from true and loving relationships with God, neighbor and creation.

Rule 1:1 is not necessarily about those people that others might judge as destined for hell or even as unfaithful. Such judgment has no place in a Christian community. All Christians have within themselves movements, inclinations, desires and tendencies that if followed will lead them away from loving relationships with God, others and creation.[3]

In describing a person one admires, one will at times encounter another person whose experience of the person described is quite different, even contrary to one's own. During such an experience, one might find oneself questioning: "Are you sure the person you are talking about is the same person I'm talking about?"

There are many reasons why this phenomenon occurs. One reason is that every person has both strengths and weaknesses. One person might experience the person in question working out of his/her strength while another might experience this same person working out of weakness.

Using Rule 1:1, one can diagram the way the dynamics of good and evil work on persons operating out of their weaknesses in this way:

Rule 1:1 Persons Operating Out of Their Weakness	
The Good Spirit	**The Evil Spirit**
The Good Spirit will sting the conscience of a person operating out of weakness and encourage a change in direction. The Good Spirit will play inner messages such as: "This kind of behavior is not helping your relationships." "You will need to get some help with your drinking, anger, lust, etc." "If you continue in this way, you will grow more and more lonely and empty."	The evil spirit will encourage a person operating out of weakness to be unreflective and uncritical about their weakness. The evil spirit will play inner messages such as: "Have some fun now and worry about your spouse, children, friends, etc., later." "Sure you drink, get angry, act lustfully, etc., but you have it under control when you want to." "Life is short. If you live it up, (meaning if you give in to your weaknesses and ignore your relationships), you will be happy."

Case Study: Ralph and Sue

Ralph and Sue have three children. They want to provide financial stability for their children and to spend quality time with them in their growing years. Sue is offered a job with a salary that will substantially lessen the financial pressure on the family, but will also require her to spend time on the road away from home. Sue and Ralph's discernment concerning this issue will need to balance their real need for greater financial resources with their values in regard to family life.

Such dilemmas rarely have an easy answer. Sue and Ralph could choose more money without seriously considering their values regarding family life, or they could choose family values and repress the need for basic financial stability. Opting for either financial security or family values without balancing the truth of both realities will probably not result in true peace.

Sue and Ralph are essentially good people. Each has strengths and weaknesses. Sue comes from a family who worked its way out of dire poverty. In her birth family she learned that money was the way to life and freedom. The evil spirit will use this weakness—it is also one of her strengths—to attempt to undermine her real concern for family life. Sue's need for financial security may cause her to minimize the importance of spending time with her family.

Ralph has a birth family that enjoys each other and values time together, but is negligent in paying bills and in being socially responsible. The evil spirit will use this inherent weakness—it is also one of Ralph's strengths—to try to undermine the value of financial responsibility.

In either case, one is looking at essentially good people with weaknesses. As was mentioned earlier, one's weakness and strength are often two sides of the same coin. Sue's strength of being financially responsible, if overstressed, can lead to irresponsibility in family relationships.

Ralph's relational strength carried to extreme can result in financial irresponsibility.

In the second part of Rule 1:1, Ignatius speaks of the dynamics of the Good Spirit. The Good Spirit challenges persons who are not being faithful in their relationships with God, neighbor and creation. If Sue chooses financial security to the extreme and neglects her family, the Good Spirit will challenge her extreme. Sue might experience tinges of conscience that remind her of the value of fostering family relationships. If Ralph enjoys his family without concern for financial stability, the Good Spirit will challenge his irresponsibility by suggesting that he be more honest about paying bills, putting in a day's work, budgeting in a realistic way, etc.

To summarize, when one is acting in a way that is not true to oneself and one's relationships with others, the evil spirit will encourage one to keep acting in this way. The Good Spirit, on the other hand, will challenge one to move toward that which truly fosters loving and honest relationships with God, neighbor and creation. Though the Good Spirit might bother consciences, the Good Spirit encourages people to be their best selves. While the evil spirit's suggestions may at times be more comfortable, its way will eventually bring confusion and emptiness.

Using Rule 1:1, one might diagram the movements of the Good Spirit and the evil spirit on Sue's weakness as follows:

Applying Rule 1:1 A Closer Look at Sue	
The Good Spirit	**The Evil Spirit**
When Sue is operating out of her weakness, the Good Spirit will oppose this direction with messages such as:	When Sue is operating out of her weakness, the evil spirit will encourage this direction with messages such as:
"You need to balance both financial security with time for fostering family relationships."	"You better take this job now. You probably won't have the chance to earn such a good salary again."
"Money isn't everything, Sue."	"Your husband can take care of the children. Its about time he did his part."
"Changing your spending habits will also affect your family's financial stability. Maybe you need to look at the option of living a simpler lifestyle."	"Family values are wonderful but sometimes you just have to be realistic. Money is really what runs the world."

Items for Reflection/Discussion

1. Diagram possible actions of the Good Spirit and the evil spirit on Ralph's weakness. Discuss.

2. Write a case study regarding a decision or circumstance you would like to reflect upon from your own life. Diagram the actions of the Good Spirit and evil spirit on your own weakness. What are the messages the

Good Spirit tends to play inside of you? What are the
messages the evil spirit plays?

3. How might it be more possible for you to consistently
follow the counsel of the Good Spirit?

❧ *Rule 1:2 Know Your Strength* ❧

Rule 1:2 describes people when they are acting in ways that
encourage true and loving relationships with God, neighbor and creation.

Rule 1:2

> In the case of persons who are earnestly purging
> away their sins, and who are progressing from
> good to better in the service of God our Lord, the
> procedure used is the opposite of that described
> in the First Rule. For in this case it is characteristic
> of the evil spirit to cause gnawing anxiety, to
> sadden, and to set up obstacles. In this way he
> unsettles them by false reasons aimed at
> preventing their progress.

> But with persons of this type it is characteristic of
> the good spirit to stir up courage and strength,
> consolations, tears, inspirations, and tranquility.
> He makes things easier and eliminates all obsta-
> cles, so that the persons may move forward in
> doing good.[4]

One can use Rule 1:2 to reflect upon good people who
are not necessarily perfect, but who are working out of their
personal strengths. In this case, the evil spirit does everything it can to discourage them through anxiety, sadness, obstacles and false reasoning. The Good Spirit, on the other hand,
brings courage, consolation, peace, and ease of movement.

In the case of Ralph and Sue, it would be characteristic
of the evil spirit to discourage their attempts to work to-

ward a solution to their dilemma. The movement of evil might exaggerate either their need for money or their desire for family values in order to sabotage the process of deliberating both concerns. It might overstate fears either of not having adequate finances or of being irresponsible parents. The Good Spirit on the other hand would encourage them in their decision-making, would remove obstacles and would offer a creative means of solving their dilemma.

One might outline the dynamics Sue may be experiencing in regard to her personal strength in this way:

Applying Rule 1:2 A Closer Look at Sue	
The Good Spirit	**The Evil Spirit**
When Sue is operating out of her strength, the Good Spirit will encourage her with messages such as:	When Sue is operating out of her strength, the evil spirit will discourage her with messages such as:
"Financial stability is an important consideration for family life. Consider this factor in light of your values regarding family relationships."	"It you take this job your children will never grow close to you. When you become old, they will abandon you just as you abandoned them."
"Might there be other ways to provide the family with financial security other than taking this job?"	"Every Christian knows that a mother's place is in the home, not running around doing business."
"It is true that financial responsibility does promote true and loving relationships. Value both financial responsibility and loving relationships."	"This obsession you have with money is just a leftover from your dysfunctional family. If bills don't get paid on time, it's no big deal."

Items for Reflection/Discussion

1. Diagram the actions of the Good Spirit and the evil spirit on Ralph's strength. Discuss.

2. Write a personal case study regarding a decision or circumstance you would like to reflect upon from your own life. Diagram the actions of the Good Spirit and the evil spirit on your own strength. What are the messages the Good Spirit tends to play inside of you? What are the messages the evil spirit plays?

3. How might it be more possible for you to consistently follow the counsel of the Good Spirit?

Summary

The first two *Rules* for Discernment offer guidance for noticing the movements of good and evil in one's life. When one is working out of weakness, the evil spirit will discourage one from working against this weakness. It will justify one's weakness by using some truth, but then exaggerating it or understating it. The Good Spirit will encourage one toward greater virtue, truth and strength of character. It will prompt one toward greater faith, hope and love in God, others and creation.

When one is working out of one's strength, the evil spirit will do everything it can to discourage one from continuing to move toward true and loving relationships. It will attempt to exaggerate how hard one is trying with how little one is accomplishing. It will try to move one toward distrust without hope and without love. It will play inner tapes such as, "You are lost." "You gave everything to God and where has it gotten you." "If you surrender to God, God will take advantage of you," etc.

The influence of the Good Spirit on the other hand will encourage one by eliminating obstacles, providing opportunities and giving peace. Its inner tapes give messages such as, "Do not be afraid." "Have courage." "Trust God."

Case Study: The Retreat Center Discussion

When Christians gather in community, every person in the group brings both strengths and weaknesses. The movements of good and evil within a group happen as these differing personalities with their strengths and weaknesses interrelate.

The case of the Retreat Center Discussion is designed to enable readers to participate in or observe a small group of Christians trying to reach a common decision. There are seven personalities that enter the discussion. The point of this exercise is to help observers and participants notice how different personalities bring both strengths and weaknesses to a group dynamic.

The Setting

Each person participating in the discussion is a member of the staff of St. Thomas Parish. The group is convening to discuss the fate of a house once used by a parish minister that is owned by the parish and is presently vacant. There has been quite a bit of previous but informal discussion about the possibility of turning the house into a parish retreat center. Eventually, the staff is to arrive at a decision; however, since this is the first formal discussion concerning the issue, it is not expected that a decision will be made at this meeting.

Directions

This case requires the participation of seven people. If your class or discussion group is larger than seven people, you might divide into a number of groups or ask some members of your group to be observers.

Each participant is to choose a particular role in the discussion. Adjust the genders of the characters as needed. Participants are to wear name tags so that they can address each other in character. Those playing roles are to do their best not to let their own personalities get in the way of their characterizations.

The group has no designated leader. The discussion simply begins after all have had the opportunity to read their roles. The role-play ends when the professor or group facilitator feels enough discussion has passed to demonstrate the relational styles of the seven characters.

The Roles

Mr. or Ms. Knowing

Your name is Knowing. You are concerned that not all the facts have been gathered and adequately considered for this project. You want to be cautious and urge the group to move slowly in their considerations.

You are concerned that the location of the parish house is not suitable for a retreat center. Since the parish house is located within the city, you wonder whether there is enough space to ensure that retreatants will have room for private reflection. This lack of space away from others concerns you.

You are interested in hearing others speak in order to identify where each staff member is in the discussion. In meetings you often speak last because you want to be sure your opinion is informed by others. Because of this, others often perceive you as wise and wait for your few words of wisdom.

Mr. or Ms. Loyalist

Your name is Loyalist. You are aware that there will be some tension in this discussion and you hope that the meeting will proceed without open conflict. You know that Pastor Bill is hoping that the team will be in favor of the retreat center, and you hope that Bill's preference will be affirmed by the group. Pastor Bill is a good friend of yours, and you want to do all you can to support his dream.

You have heard that the Social Justice Advocate in the group has other plans for the parish house, and you hope to cool down support for the Social Justice Advocate's position. You prefer to be more realistic and desire to draw the group into common support of a project, rather than divide the group and in the end accomplish nothing.

You have brought coffee and cookies for the meeting and are concerned that everyone is physically and psychologically comfortable.

Mr. or Ms. Social Justice Advocate

Your name is Social Justice Advocate. As usual, you hold the minority position on the issue in question, but you feel that someone continually needs to challenge the staff's fidelity to Christian values. It seems to you that a retreat center is not a responsible choice for a parish that is located in a city full of homeless people.

You strongly try to make the point that the parish would receive many more blessings if it used the parish house as a homeless shelter. Other parishes have done such things, and civil agencies are in need of more shelter space. You wonder how the staff can think selfishly of their own private needs when basic needs of food, clothing and shelter for their neighbors are not being met. You feel that you are witnessing the story of Dives and Lazarus in a contemporary setting.

You know that you will have to state your position strongly in the group, since it is a minority position, and the poor have only your voice to speak for them. You are disgusted with those who want to move forward with Pastor Bill's idea of the retreat center. You feel these people would rather agree with whatever an authority figure says rather than take their civil and Christian responsibilities seriously. For the sake of the poor, you are willing to unmask the hypocrisy of those who would choose a socially irresponsible option.

Mr. or Ms. Cool

Your name is Cool. You are willing to do whatever the group thinks is best in coming to a decision about the parish house. However, you do hope that the group doesn't get upset in the process. It just isn't worth a hassle. Life will go on with or without a retreat center.

You do all you can when things get a bit tense in the group to bring the group back to balance. Nothing will get done if there isn't peace, and getting something done isn't always what is most important in life. There might be moments during the discussion when you sit back and think to yourself that you'd rather be home watching television and eating pizza. Only a few more hours and then you can go home.

When you contribute to the discussion, you tend to tell stories and to ramble on in a kind of unimpassioned monotone. This kind of lulling does neutralize the emotion experienced by the group. Although most will not be able to connect directly with what you are saying, you are a likeable person and your stories are interesting. After speaking you can again think about the pizza you will have after the meeting.

Mr. or Ms. Inspector

You name is Inspector. You are willing to consider the possibility of the retreat center but feel that Pastor Bill, as usual, is not attending to details necessary to the project.

Although you do not want to appear openly disrespectful, you wish Pastor Bill would become a bit more organized. Some of the other people on the committee are also irritating you. In fact it seems that most of the staff members are not too competent, but you bear with it and try to keep people on track by choice comments here and there that call them back to reality.

You are concerned about details of the project that no one else has considered. For instance, will there be zoning problems in turning the parish house over to another use? Has the parish considered the cost of remodeling and estimated revenue potential? Are there already too many retreat centers in the area that are in financial difficulty?, etc.

Mr. or Ms. Worker

Your name is Worker. You are very interested in the retreat center project and have many ideas as to how you might offer your skills to make this dream a reality. You can see how much work the building needs and would like to start remodeling as soon as possible.

You are already making plans to cook for retreats on your free weekends. This will save the parish some money, and you enjoy cooking.

If you have any hesitation, it lies in the fact that you have given hours of extra time and service to the parish, and this has not always been appreciated. Even so, you are mature enough to look at the bigger picture of service. You are eager and want to get started.

Mr. or Ms. Artist

Your name is Artist. You love the idea of a retreat center because you feel that the inner life of people in the parish community is given so little attention. You look forward to having the retreat center on the parish grounds so that you can regularly take time apart from the pressures of work and family.

You went over to the parish house yesterday and began dreaming of possibilities for the interior design of the house. You have many ideas for a creative use of space and for a contemplative mix of colors.

You wait for someone to acknowledge the need for your creative talents. You certainly have demonstrated how uniquely talented you are in smaller projects like liturgical environment and in the interior design of the parish offices.

If no one is understanding enough to acknowledge and call forth your talents, you softly express your interest in using your gifts for this project. You do this only once, since if the group doesn't have the wisdom to acknowledge its need of you, it really doesn't deserve to benefit from your gifts.

Questions for Reflection/Discussion

1. What gifts do each of the personalities bring to the discussion? How might the Good Spirit use the goodness of each of these personalities?

2. What weaknesses do each of the personalities bring to the discussion? How might the evil spirit use these weaknesses for its own purpose?

3. How might one's weakness become one's strength?

4. With all these differing personalities, how might a Christian community come to a peaceful solution?

5. If you were an outsider asked to facilitate a group discernment regarding the use of the parish house, what process would you suggest?

Suggestion for Further Reading

Toner, Jules. "The Fundamental Principles for Discerning Spirits: Rules I:1-2." Chap. in *A Commentary on Saint Ignatius' Rules for the Discernment of Spirits*. St. Louis: The Institute of Jesuit Sources, 1982. Toner's work is a scholarly commentary on the *Rules for Discernment*. His contrast of "concrete complexities in contrast to pure cases" and his illustration of this complexity using the case study of the rich young man (Mk 10:17-22) is a valuable aid to a beginner trying to understand the nuances of the first two *Rules*.

6

Is It Only Just a Mood?

❧ ☙

Inner and Outer Movements

Case Study: Bill

One evening Bill receives a call. His uncle Jim has died. Jim was an old man and the call does not leave Bill surprised. Jim's funeral service is Monday night. Bill is scheduled to work Monday night.

Bill did not know uncle Jim very well, so he decides that it is not necessary for him to go to Jim's service. One hour later, his mother calls. Bill forgot how kind his uncle Jim had been to his mother through the years. A little while later his cousin calls and asks if Bill would serve as a pallbearer for the funeral. Bill finds himself saying that he will need to check to see if he can be excused from work. He calls his boss and arranges alternate hours.

In this simple event many inner and outer movements are affecting Bill's relationships. His initial decision not to ask for time away from work to go to the funeral seems grounded in reason. He did not know uncle Jim well. His mother's phone call, however, puts that decision in a different perspective. Although he did not know his uncle Jim well, he wants to honor a man who respected his mother. Finally his cousin's request moves him to call his boss to arrange alternate hours.

In this simple scenario many lives and relationships are interconnected. Bill's decision affects his relationship with his mother, his cousin, his employer and many others who will attend the funeral. Although he is not moved to attend

Jim's funeral in response to his relationship with Jim, he later attends because of his relationship with his family.

One's daily life is filled with inner and outer movements which affect how one relates with others. People who notice these movements are better able to name and understand what is happening in their lives.

Outer Movements

When attempting to choose the Holy Spirit in the midst of daily life, it is important to pay attention to outer movements. These movements include such things as facts, financial resources, popular opinions and biases, personal health, opportunities, educational certifications, deadlines, political climate, etc. In sum, outer movements are external influencing factors such as events, opportunities, resources, etc., which affect people as they relate with God, others and the world.

Not long ago a parasite infected the water supply of a large American city. The tiny organism passed through the city's filtration system unnoticed. As schools, businesses and offices closed because of the sickness the parasite caused, the attention of an entire city focused on this tiny organism. The city was forced to admit its dependence upon the earth and its resources. The invasion of the tiny organism had financial implications, social implications and challenged attitudes toward environmental issues. The parasite and the havoc it caused were "outer movements" that demanded to be noticed.

The Gospel reminds Christians that they are to "be wise as serpents and innocent as doves" (Mt 10:16). Those who do not pay attention to the movements happening around them fail to grasp the possibilities and limitations of their human creaturehood that is interdependent with other human persons and with the cosmos.

Case Study: Julie

Julie is a 32-year-old woman. She is single but only because she has not yet found the right person to marry. She does community nursing and works with mothers and children who are at risk. For recreation she enjoys team sports such as volleyball and baseball.

One evening, Julie is coming home from a talk on the politics of health care, when a car runs a stoplight and hits her broadside. Three days later, Julie wakes up and learns that she is paralyzed below her waist. Her legs are completely shattered and the doctors feel that they may need to amputate both of them.

Julie is weak and heavily medicated. She insists that the doctors are wrong and that she will be walking and playing ball again. She tries repeatedly to get out of bed and eventually needs to be tied down. At times she starts to cry uncontrollably and she feels like she wants to die.

Julie will most likely need much physical, psychological and spiritual help as she learns to accept the consequences of her unfortunate accident. During this process there are some facts that she will need to accept: She did have an accident; the accident will most likely leave permanent physical damage; it is very likely that this damage will affect her ability to work and to play sports in the same way she has in the past. There are cases in which people with strong wills have beaten the odds, but life also often deals hard facts that must be faced. In noticing the facts and in attempting to understand them, Julie will be better able to make decisions regarding her future.

Inner Movements

Inner movements such as moods, tendencies, desires, inclinations, passions, feelings, attractions, impulses, etc., are also important to one's growth in relationships. One chooses not only the outer course of one's life, but also one's inner direction.

All persons are subject to moods, tendencies, affections, inclinations, desires and passions. Of themselves these natural movements are part of what it means to be a human person. Some of these movements happen quite spontaneously, and the person does well simply to notice their existence. Others can be encouraged or discouraged.

Neglecting to pay attention to inner movements can invite disaster. A father who is out of touch with his own feelings of failure might bully his son with unrealistic expectations. As the son matures, he may be forced to reject his father in order to grow into his own person. The father is alienated and abandoned and feels as though he has failed again. If someone could have helped the father notice his own insecurity and guided him toward becoming more interiorly secure, the father perhaps could have related to his son more effectively.

One's inner movements affect the way one relates to others and to the world. If one is out of touch with one's own spirit, one relates in shallow and manipulative ways.

Consolation and Desolation

❧ Rule 1:3 Identify Consolation ❧

In Rules 1:3 and 4 of the *Rules for Discernment*, Ignatius refers to the terms "consolation" and "desolation." Ignatius uses these terms in a specific sense.

Rules 1:3 and 4 take seriously daily outer events and inner movements that affect human relationships. Ignatius invites the one who is striving to be loving and truthful in relationships, to separate those movements that tend toward greater faith, hope and love of God, others and the world from those movements that promote distrust, despair and apathy.

Rule 1:3

> By consolation I mean that which occurs when
> some interior motion is caused within the soul
> through which it comes to be inflamed with love
> of its Creator and Lord. As a result it can love no
> created thing on the face of the earth in itself, but
> only in the Creator of them all.
>
> Similarly, this consolation is experienced when
> the soul sheds tears which move it to love for its
> Lord—whether they are tears of grief for its own
> sins, or about the Passion of Christ our Lord, or
> about other matters directly ordered to his service
> and praise.
>
> Finally, under the word consolation I include
> every increase in hope, faith, and charity, and
> every interior joy which calls and attracts one to-
> ward heavenly things and to the salvation of one's
> soul, by bringing it tranquility and peace in its
> Creator and Lord.[1]

Ignatius speaks of three manifestations of the consolation he is trying to describe. First, consolation is a movement of the soul that moves a person to love God and others
more deeply. God's relationship with each person is one
grounded in truth and in love. As they enter relationships,
human persons try to love as God first has loved them—in
truth and in tenderness.

The discerning person strives to love others in truth
and in love rather than with tainted motives or selfish
projections. When a person is not holding on to false
"loves"—"loves" which are not grounded in truth and in
love—then one is free to surrender one's heart to another.

Love of God and love of neighbor and all things is
more than fleeting affection. Love is an enduring act of the
will. One proves one's love for God and others not only
by waxing poetically about one's love, but by deciding to
place oneself at the service of the other.

It is possible to love another and yet feel desolate in spirit. A mother with three children in diapers and a father who works two jobs to support the family will most likely feel naturally desolate at times though they are doing all they can to persevere in love for each other and for their children. At times the feelings of love leave them and they are left only with the will to persevere as a family.

Ignatius would call the couple's fidelity to each other and their children "consolation" even though on a feeling level they might be experiencing "desolation." Consolation for Ignatius is that movement within relationships that prompts fidelity in faith, hope and love. Sometimes one chooses to be faithful in spite of discouragement or frustration.

It is a tremendous gift when God inflames the heart in one's relationship with another or while one is in prayer. The consolation of the experience of God's love or of the love of another person can sustain one through times when love feels more like an exercise in fidelity than an affection.

Second, Ignatius speaks of the consolation of tears. Tears can be tears of contrition or a recognition of one's personal weakness. One might in good faith perform an action that causes hurt to another. Since tears can lead to greater personal insight and resolution to act differently in the future, weeping over one's lack of love can be a movement toward consolation even though one might feel naturally miserable. One might weep over the Passion of Christ as it is suffered in the poor and oppressed today. Tears might also be shed over daily matters in which one is trying one's best to follow the lead of the Holy Spirit. Sometimes life just falls apart. One is sorry that one cannot do things better; that one cannot seem to make a difference. If one's tears lead to a greater desire to love, then Ignatius would speak of them as tears of consolation.

Finally, and perhaps most importantly, Ignatius sees consolation as any movement that inspires one to greater faith, hope, love and joy. Even if one is going through a very difficult period in one's life, if one's suffering leads to greater faith, hope and love towards one's neighbor and God, it can be spoken of in Ignatian terms as consolation.

Consolation as Joy

In the third *Rule*, Ignatius describes consolation as "every increase in hope, faith and charity, and every interior joy." The joy Ignatius speaks of is not a giddy type of happiness but rather a foundational joy that prepares one for the peaceful existence of heavenly life with God and with others.[2] There is a firm conviction that accompanies this joy that all shall be well.[3]

Embracing suffering in the Christian life is difficult. Most Christians are like the apostles who ran away from the crucified Jesus. It is difficult to hold in one's person the tensions of the cross: the tension between the desire to speak about the love of God and the reality of horrible human suffering; the tension between the need to have organization in religion and the impulse to follow the lead of the Spirit; the tension between the human need for beautiful ritual and the hunger for simple, unaffected prayer. It is easy to reject elements of tension which one prefers to ignore. It is difficult to hang on to the tensions of human life and to enter into the pain of Calvary.

If embracing the tensions of the cross is difficult, choosing joy is more difficult. Heaven demands much of its residents. One must possess a mature peace and a tranquil spirit to be happy with heavenly joy.

In a famous story, St. Francis is pictured speaking to Brother Leo about the difficulty of choosing joy. Francis tells Leo that if the world's best theologians became Franciscans, that would not be true joy. He goes on to say that if all the clergy and archbishops became Franciscans, that would not be true joy. If his brothers converted the nonbelievers or performed many miracles, that would not be true joy.

Brother Leo rightfully exclaims: "What then is true joy?" Francis responds:

I return from Perugia and arrive here in the dead of night; and it is winter time, muddy and so cold that icicles have formed on the edges of my habit and keep striking my legs, and blood flows from such wounds. And all covered with mud and cold, I come to the gate and after I have knocked and called for some time, a brother comes and asks: 'Who are you?' I answer: 'Brother Francis.' And he says: 'Go away; this is not a proper hour for going about; you may not come in.' And when I insist, he answers: 'Go away, you are a simple and a stupid person; we are so many and we have no need of you. You are certainly not coming to us at this hour!' And I stand again at the door and say: 'For the love of God, take me in tonight.' And he answers: 'I will not. Go to the Crosiers' place and ask there.' I tell you this: If I had patience and did not become upset, there would be true joy in this and true virtue and the salvation of the soul.[4]

When feelings of affection, goodness and peace join with an assurance that one is following the Spirit of God, there is joy. Francis is speaking here, however, of a joy that perseveres in peace even when those who should be loving one do one harm. Although Francis might be physically miserable, if he has patience and peace through his ordeal, then he truly is in consolation.

An old grandfather once had seven grandchildren whom he deeply loved. One of them became ill with brain cancer when he was just three years old. The grandfather stayed at the child's side playing checkers with him when he was feeling better and holding his hand when he was full of pain. When the child died, the grandfather's heart felt as though it were breaking with grief. Wondering how the old man would survive his anguish, a hospital chaplain spoke to the grandfather, asking if he still believed in God in the face of such tragedy. Without hesitating the grandfather replied that he had lived a long time and had learned that God is faithful. His tears were full of grief and anguish at the death of his young grandson, but they were not tears of despair.

Those who truly love others and God feel the world's suffering most keenly. Perhaps this is why Ignatius cannot separate tears from consolation. In consolation, pain and joy are reconciled. The grandfather's heart, broken with grief, still believed and loved his God. Francis' heart, saddened by his brothers' lack of love, remained in peace.

To summarize, one can identify consolation as any movement that leads one to greater faith, hope and love in God, others and creation and every interior joy. It is a movement that brings together the tensions of life and harmonizes these tensions within the heart and mind of a person. This holding of the world's tensions as core to one's spiritual journey, crucifies one with Christ and initiates one into the depths of joy. At times one's natural desires, tendencies, inclinations and passions intensify the experience of consolation. At other times consolation is experienced as the quiet and tranquil peace and joy that upholds one even as one weeps.

❧ Rule 1:4 Identify Desolation ❧

Rule 1:4

> By desolation I mean everything which is the contrary of what was described in the Third Rule; for example, darkness of soul, turmoil within it, an impulsive motion toward low and earthly things, or disquiet from various agitations and temptations. These move one toward lack of faith and leave one without hope and without love. One is completely listless, tepid, and unhappy, and feels separated from our Creator and Lord.
>
> For just as consolation is contrary to desolation, so too the thoughts which arise from consolation

are likewise contrary to those which spring from desolation.[5]

Ignatius describes desolation as the contrary of consolation. Desolation leads one away from God into confusion, without faith, hope or love. Desolation leaves one isolated, unhappy and listless.

Confusion is key in identifying desolation. When one is confused, it is difficult to sort through one's inner thoughts, moods, desires and inclinations. It is also difficult to evaluate external facts, opinions and opportunities. This confusion can tempt one to distrust God and others.

Desolation of itself is not necessarily the fault of the person in desolation. Of themselves spontaneous movements of consolation and desolation within a person are not blameworthy or praiseworthy. One does not blame oneself for being in a bad mood, unless one deliberately tries to be in a bad mood or does nothing to get out of the bad mood. One is not responsible for spontaneous lustful thoughts, unless one encourages such thoughts. Thoughts, affections, tendencies, feelings, inclinations and desires are essential to what it means to be a human person. Without these inner movements, life would be very dull. Given these inner movements, human persons have the capacity to make choices continually as they foster relationship with God, others and the world.

In summary, desolation undermines one's desire for relationship through degrees of discouragement and confusion. Of itself desolation is morally neutral. If people succumb to its movement toward apathy and despair, they move into isolation. If people struggle against the desolation and do all they can to persevere in faith, hope, love and joy, then the struggle against desolation becomes a movement towards greater faith, hope, love and joy in God, others and the world.

Case Study: Tony Goes to College

Tony is a high school senior and an honor student. His plan is eventually to go on to medical school. He is excited about beginning college and feels energized though applying to a number of schools requires filling out countless forms.

Tony's younger sister, Ann, has Down's syndrome. She also has had several serious bouts of pneumonia that have weakened her lungs. Tony and Ann are close, and whenever Tony thinks about leaving Ann to go away to school, he feels sad. Ann does not seem to understand that Tony will be leaving home. She tells people that Tony is her best friend and that he will never leave her. Tony tries to tell Ann that he needs to leave for school, but will see her some weekends and during vacations. Ann does not want to hear this.

Tony's guidance counselor, Jim, notices that a prestigious university is offering five scholarships to potential pre-med students. After sending for more information, he asks Tony if he would be interested. Tony, whose highest ambition was the state university, is thrilled. He fills out the forms and mails them the next day. He does not think that he has a realistic chance for a scholarship, but he knows that applying for it will be a good experience.

After a series of interviews and more paperwork, Tony receives a call telling him that he has received a full four-year scholarship. Tony is stunned. He never thought that he would actually be chosen. He goes downstairs to tell his mother and father.

During supper, Tony's father opens some wine and invites Tony to share his news with the family. After the announcement, Ann breaks down in tears. She would not talk with anyone. Tony feels terrible.

Later, before he falls asleep, Tony asks himself if he really wants to go so far away to school. Maybe he will not like medicine. Maybe people will make fun of his

Midwest accent. Perhaps living on a university campus will be hard for someone who is from a country town.

When Tony thinks of Ann, he becomes even more confused. He has tried hard never to let her down. Now he is leaving her. If he went to the state university, he could be home with her more often. Who knows how long Ann will live? Maybe he will be wasting precious time that he should spend closer to his sister. Maybe leaving Ann to go to school is nothing other than a selfish ambition.

Confused and frustrated, Tony tries to pray. He tells God about the situation. He knows that a full scholarship to such a prestigious university is something most people would give anything for. Yet, he wonders if his motive for leaving Ann is a good one. It is true that he wants to be a genetic researcher and dedicate his life to the study of Down's Syndrome, but who knows if that dream will actually materialize? Tony feels overwhelmed, and his prayer offers him no relief.

The next morning Tony feels better. He spends time asking God to show him what he should do. He decides to see his guidance counselor to ask for more information and to talk about his confusion about leaving Ann. Feeling more peaceful, he goes downstairs for breakfast.

Consolation and Desolation in the Case of Tony

It is important to realize that Ignatius' *Rules* will not offer Tony a quick and easy answer. The purpose of the *Rules* is to help one notice, in order that one might understand, so that one might act.

Sometimes it is helpful to chart the movements of consolation (those external facts, shifts in relationships, impulses, thoughts and feelings that tend toward greater faith, hope and love of God, others and the world) and desolation (those external facts, shifts in relationships, impulses, thoughts and feelings that tend towards mistrust, despair and apathy towards God, others and the world).

The following outline notes facts and movements in Tony's life. These are charted as desolation or consolation according to the most probable response one might have to the fact or movement in question. For instance, the fact of Ann's Down's syndrome is listed as a desolation. Down's syndrome is usually seen as a hardship, as something that challenges a family.

In the same way, Tony and Ann's relationship is charted as a consolation. Although this relationship is causing them both pain at the moment (desolation), most would see the respect and love Tony and Ann have for each other as a valuable treasure (consolation). The struggles Tony and Ann are experiencing over the issue of Tony going away to school are charted as desolation.

There is a value in charting one's initial response to a situation. Once one notices and names the consolations and desolations involved, then one can note how these movements change over time. If Tom charts his consolations and desolations in regard to another life experience a year later, he might gain much insight from comparing his reactions with those recorded below.

Applying Rules 1:3-4
A Closer Look at Tony

Consolation (That which can move one to greater faith, hope and love in God, others and the world)	Desolation (That which can move one to distrust, despair and apathy toward God, others and the world).
Fact: Tony is doing well in school. **Feeling:** Tony feels "excited and energized" about going to college. **Relationship:** Tony and Ann have a "close" relationship. **Feeling:** Tony is initially "thrilled" about applying for the scholarship. **Fact:** Tony receives a full four-year scholarship. **Relationships:** Tony's parents seem happy about Tony's opportunity. **Relationship:** Tony's father breaks open a bottle of wine to celebrate. **Relationship:** Tony prays. **Relationship:** Tony's love for Ann seems to be prompting him to dedicate his life to the study of Down's syndrome. **Feeling:** Tony feels more "peaceful" in the morning. **Action:** Tony's processing leads him to action—he goes to see the guidance counselor again.	**Fact:** Tony's sister, Ann, has Down's syndrome and her lungs are weakened from pneumonia. **Feeling:** Tony is "sad" whenever he thinks about leaving Ann. **Fact:** Ann does not seem to understand Tony's leaving. **Fact:** Ann tells people that Tony will never leave her. **Fact:** Ann breaks down in tears. She will not talk with anyone. **Feeling:** Tony feels "terrible." **Inner Questions:** Tony wonders whether it is good for him to accept the scholarship. **Feeling:** Tony becomes "confused" when he thinks of Ann and he questions his motivations. **Fact:** Ann may not live long. **Fact:** There is a chance that Tony's dream of becoming a genetic researcher will not materialize even if he does go away to school. **Relationship:** Tony's prayer gives him no comfort.

Case Study: Grandma Anna

Grandma Anna is a first generation Hungarian immigrant. She came to the United States as a young child, worked her way through high school, and married a carpenter. She has five children who are now married with children of their own.

Grandma Anna is one of those persons who is willing to help with whatever needs to be done. When someone dies from the parish, Grandma Anna is there to serve the funeral dinner. When her grandchildren need a baby-sitter, Grandma Anna comes to care for them. When clothing is collected for the poor, Grandma Anna takes soiled items home and washes and irons them. She seems to do everything with a twinkle in her eye. Nothing is too much for her. She goes about her daily tasks with joy and peace.

Grandma Anna does not have a lot to say about her prayer life. She reads from the Gospels every day and spends time reflecting on the life of Jesus. She regularly attends church services and is active in her parish.

Two weeks ago Grandma Anna went to the doctor for her yearly physical. The doctor discovered a lump on her neck. X-rays and a biopsy confirmed that Grandma Anna had advanced cancer. Once the diagnosis was made, Grandma Anna deteriorated rapidly.

A hospital chaplain visited Grandma Anna three days after she had been diagnosed. Grandma Anna was not herself. She was very tired, a bit cranky and said she was angry that God was taking her life so quickly when she still had many things to accomplish. She found that she did not have the energy or the interest to pray. When the chaplain began to pray with her, she asked him to leave the room.

A week later the same chaplain came back to see Grandma Anna. She was very sick, but the old twinkle was back in her eye. She apologized to the chaplain for her rudeness and told him that God and she had worked things out. When the chaplain asked if it would be helpful if he prayed with her, Grandma Anna asked him to read the passage from Matthew about the lilies of the field (Mt 6:25-34). Before the chaplain finished, Grandma Anna fell peacefully asleep.

Questions for Reflection/Discussion

1. What would you identify as movements of consolation in this case?
2. What would you identify as movements of desolation in this case?

Summary

The purpose of Ignatius' *Rules for Discernment* is to help one to:

```
┌──────────────────────────────────────────────────────────────┐
│                                                                │
│  Perceive in order to ──→ Understand in order to ──→Take       │
│                                                Appropriate     │
│                                                Action          │
│                                                                │
└──────────────────────────────────────────────────────────────┘
```

Rules 1:3 and 4 help one to notice inner and outer movements and identify them as tending towards greater faith, hope and love in God, others and the world (consolation) or away from these relationships (desolation).

Perceiving and understanding inner and outer movements helps one know how to act in ways that foster true and loving relationships. Since consolation and desolation are movements that are part of the human condition, one needs to learn how to respond to both consolation and desolation in ways that promote relationships grounded in truth and love. Ignatius offers suggestions for such action in the *Rules* discussed in the following chapters.

Suggestions for Further Reading

Lonsdale, David, S.J. "Consolation and Desolation." In *Listening to the Music of the Spirit*, 67-93. Notre Dame, IN: Ave Maria Press, 1992. Lonsdale outlines Ignatius' concepts of consolation and desolation and illustrates these ideas through pastoral case studies. He also explores different types of consolation and desolation.

Toner, Jules, S.J. "Spiritual Consolation and Desolation: Preliminary Analyses—Rules I:3 and 4," "The Description of Spiritual Consolation—Rules I:3," and "The Description of Spiritual Desolation—Rules I:4." In *A Commentary on Saint Ignatius' Rules for the Discernment of Spirits*, 79-144. St. Louis: The Institute of Jesuit Sources, 1982. Toner's scholarly commentary is required reading for any serious student of discernment of spirits.

7

Strategizing the Blues

Rules for Working Against Desolation

One is in desolation when one is discouraged, confused, unfocused and lacking in faith, hope and love. Desolation leads to unhappiness, sloth and lack of action. Little by little it can turn one away from loving and truthful relationships. Good people can be turned away from goodness if their desire for God is whittled away bit by bit.

Ignatius recognized that the movement of desolation, although morally neutral by itself, has the potential to eventually wear down the human spirit. It seemed important to him that Christians learn to work against desolation. Ignatius offers Rules 1:5-14 as guides for strategizing the blues.

Rule 1:5 Keep Things Stable

Rule 1:5

> During a time of desolation one should never make a change. Instead, one should remain firm and constant in the proposals and in a decision in which one was on the day before the desolation, or in a decision in which one was during a previous time of consolation.
>
> For just as the good spirit is chiefly the one who guides and counsels us in time of consolation, so

it is the evil spirit who does this in time of desolation. By following his counsels we can never find
the way to a right decision.[1]

Making a decision when one is discouraged, tepid,
depressed and lacking in faith, hope and love is ill-advised.
The reason, Ignatius explains, is that the movement happening in one's heart during a time of desolation is not a
movement that is leading one toward God and others.
Making a premature decision in a moment of desolation is
generally not a good idea. Ignatius advises persons in
desolation to hold on to the decisions they made when they
were in consolation.

Patrick is a person tempted to make a decision during
a time of desolation. Patrick is a young social worker who
for the last two years has been working in a homeless
shelter. For as long as Patrick can remember he has desired
to work in social services. He finds that his work is re-
warding and that it is a way for him to live out his commitment to love those who are poor.

Lately, however, Patrick is discouraged. On weekends he enjoys sailing and wishes that he could earn enough
money to buy himself a sailboat. Many of his high school
friends who went on to school for business or law degrees
have made more money than Patrick and have more afflu-
ent lifestyles. Although Patrick does not have the desire
for all the things they have, he really would like a sailboat.

Patrick finds himself becoming more and more impa-
tient with those who come to the shelter. One night he
begins to think about quitting his job to take a position
with higher compensation.

Questions for Reflection/Discussion

1. Using the first four *Rules for Discernment*, how would you
   describe Patrick's state of mind and heart? Does he seem
   to be moving towards his best self or is he getting hooked?
   Is he in consolation or in desolation?

2. Would you advise Patrick to give up his job without further discernment? Is this the time for him to be making a decision?

❧ *Rule 1:6 Change Yourself* ☙

Although making significant changes during times of desolation is not recommended, Rule 1:6 follows the Christian tradition by recommending that one counter desolation through prayer, self-examination and penance. While prayer and self-examination help one to reflect upon one's inner and outer responses in light of God's love, penance moves one contrary to the desolation one is experiencing. If one is desolate because one is overindulgent, then fasting may bring peace. If one is burnt out, play and relaxation might restore wholeness.

Rule 1:6

> It is taken for granted that in time of desolation we ought not to change our former plans. But it is very helpful to make vigorous changes in ourselves as counterattack against the desolation, for example, by insisting more on prayer, meditation, earnest self-examination, and some suitable way of doing penance.[2]

❧ *Rule 1:7 Prove Yourself* ☙

Christians who struggle to take Christianity seriously soon discover that it is not a religion suited to spiritual wimps. Christians profess to become like Christ both in their external actions and in their internal thoughts, desires, passions and inclinations. When one is in desolation, one has the opportunity to test one's inner stamina.

Rule 1:7

> When we are in desolation we should think that
> the Lord has left us in order to test us, by leaving
> us to our own natural powers so that we may prove
> ourselves by resisting the various agitations and
> temptations of the enemy. For we can do this with
> God's help, which always remains available, even
> if we do not clearly perceive it. Indeed, even
> though the Lord has withdrawn from us his abun-
> dant fervor, augmented love, and intensive grace,
> he still supplies sufficient grace for our eternal
> salvation.[3]

Even if Christians do all they can to move contrary to
desolation, there is no act of will, no penance, no work,
which can earn consolation. Consolation is a gift freely
given by God. In moving contrary to desolation, one
chooses not to cooperate with evil. One continues to trust
in the presence and love of God and others even when the
consolation of this presence is not felt.

❧ Rule 1:8 Strive to Be Patient ❧

One way to move against desolation is simply to be patient
while one is going through it. Christians need to do all they
can to counteract desolation but, when everything seems
to fail, a Christian keeps up the struggle simply by patiently
persevering in faith, hope and love.

Rule 1:8

> One who is in desolation should strive to preserve
> himself or herself in patience. This is the coun-
> terattack against the vexations which are being
> experienced. One should remember that after a
> while the consolation will return again, through

the diligent efforts against the desolation which were indicated in the Sixth Rule.[4]

By persevering in doing everything possible to move in a direction contrary to desolation, one perseveres in faith, hope and love of God and others. In this way one keeps choosing the Holy Spirit even when it seems God has abandoned one. One is tested in desolation but perseveres in patience despite the odds. Those moving against desolation believe, hope and love God and others even in the faithless, hopeless and loveless moment.

In contemplating the mystery of God's allowing desolation for a person's growth in faith, hope and love, one must be clear that God does not instigate desolation. Desolation is the tendency toward doubt, despair and apathy. This tendency cannot have God as its source. God allows desolation, but God is not the instigator of desolation.

Human experience teaches that love is purified not only in good times but also through difficulties. Hardship can be a tool for growth. A loving parent might allow a son or daughter to reap the consequences of a bad choice not for lack of love but because of love. Yet, loving parents do not deliberately will evil to happen to their children. Hardship can be used as a maturing element, as a purifying element. If one testifies that God is love, then one must also believe that hardship is tempered and fashioned by the hand of love. In the midst of trial this belief is purified.

❧ Rule 1:9 Identify the Cause of Desolation ❧

Diagnosing the cause of desolation helps one work against it. By understanding why one is desolate, one may be better able to move contrary to desolation. Ignatius offers three reasons why people might find themselves under the pall of desolation.

Rule 1:9

> There are three main reasons for the desolation
> we experience.
>
> The first is that we ourselves are tepid, lazy, or
> negligent in our spiritual exercises. Thus the
> spiritual consolation leaves us because of our own
> faults.
>
> The second reason is that the desolation serves to test
> how much we are worth, that is, how far we will go
> in the service and praise of God, even without much
> compensation by way of consolations and increased
> graces.
>
> The third reason is to give us a true recognition
> and understanding, in order to make us perceive
> interiorly that we cannot by ourselves bring on or
> retain increased devotion, intense love, tears, or any
> other spiritual consolation; and further, that all these
> are a gift and grace from God our Lord; and still
> further, that they are granted to keep us from build-
> ing our nest in a house which belongs to Another,
> by puffing up our minds with pride or vainglory
> through which we attribute the devotion or other
> features of spiritual consolation to ourselves.[5]

Ignatius claims that desolation can happen for three
reasons. First, one may be guilty of negligence or tepidity
in prayer, in moving toward balance in one's life, or in
charity toward others. When in desolation it is good to
examine oneself.

A second reason for desolation is the strengthening of
one's love for God by trial. In trial one can learn to love God
rather than the consolations God gives. As in all committed
love, God too must be loved through good and bad times.

A third reason for desolation is to teach one that consolation is a gift of God. Consolation cannot be controlled
or manipulated. Human beings cannot save themselves.

Patrick is still struggling with desolation but would probably understand it better if he studied its causes. Patrick works through the night at the homeless shelter and comes home exhausted. He tries to fall asleep but all he can think about is how unfair it is that certain professions are paid well while others like social work are less profitable. He argues with God announcing that it is time someone else does God's dirty work. He complains that he is tired of working with sick and smelly people. He informs God that he will be quitting his job as soon as he can find a job that will pay him a real salary.

Feeling better after telling God off, Patrick begins to think about all the good people he has met in his job. He realizes that the professionals he works with are wonderful people and some are becoming good friends. He remembers Tim, a homeless man, who died on the street a couple of weeks ago. Patrick really loved Tim and begins to cry at the thought of him. The memory of Tim's death makes the pain associated with his work all the more poignant. In business one does not have to go through the constant grief of becoming close to people and then attending their funerals.

Questions for Reflection/Discussion

1. How would you describe the movements of consolation and desolation working in Patrick?

2. How might Patrick work against the desolation that he is experiencing?

3. What might be some of the causes of Patrick's desolation?

❧ Rule 1:10 Prepare for Desolation ❧

Sometimes one's greatest defense against desolation is preparation. "Prevention rather than cure" is a maxim that has great benefits for the Christian life. Ignatius believes in the value of preparation.

Rule 1:10

> One who is in consolation should consider how
> he or she will act in future desolation, and store
> up new strength for that time.[6]

One of the most effective ways of moving against desolation is by preparing for it during times of consolation.
When one is in consolation, one sees more clearly and with
less confusion. Strengthening one's heart during times of
consolation renders times of desolation easier to bear.

❧ Rule 1:11 Move Toward Balance ☙

Ignatius summarizes his advice for struggling against desolation with the principle of balance. When one is in consolation, it is wise to prepare for desolation. In this way
one avoids the pitfall of attributing the grace of consolation
to one's own merits. In times of desolation, it is best to
prepare one's heart for consolation. In this way one keeps
alive one's hope in God.

Rule 1:11

> One who is in consolation ought to humble and
> abase himself or herself as much as possible, and
> reflect how little he or she is worth in time of deso-
> lation when that grace or consolation is absent.
>
> In contrast, one who is in desolation should reflect
> that with the sufficient grace already available he
> or she can do much to resist all hostile forces, by
> drawing strength from our Creator and Lord.[7]

❧ Rule 1:12 Be Bold ☙

Rule 1:12 betrays the gender bias of a sixteenth-century
male. The *Rule* is included here despite the gender bias in
an attempt to discover the point Ignatius is making:

Rule 1:12

> The enemy conducts himself like a woman. He is
> weak against physical strength but strong when
> confronted by weakness.
>
> When she is quarreling with a man and he shows
> himself bold and unyielding, she charac-
> teristically loses her spirit and goes away. But if
> the man begins to lose his spirit and backs away,
> the woman's anger, vindictiveness, and ferocity
> swell almost without limit.
>
> In the same way, the enemy characteristically weak-
> ens, loses courage, and flees with his temptations
> when the person engaged in spiritual endeavors
> stands bold and unyielding against the enemy's
> temptations and goes diametrically against them.
> But if, in contrast, that person begins to fear and
> lose courage in the face of the temptations, there is
> no beast on the face of the earth as fierce as the
> enemy of human nature when he is pursuing his
> damnable intention with his surging malice.[8]

Ignatius' point is that Christians who prepare for desolation and act against it must also be bold when confronted
by evil. Those who are caught unprepared, unfortified,
and yield in weakness are prime targets for evil. For them,
evil shows no mercy desolating their spirits and eroding
their hope.

Ignatius' message is clear. Those who wish to live the
Christian life need to learn how to work against desolation.
To do this they need to know themselves and their vulnerabilities. They also need to realize that evil has no compas-
sion regarding their weakness. Their protection is to be
prepared and to be bold.

❧ *Rule 1:13 Bring Secrets Into the Light* ❧

Another tactic of the evil spirit is secrecy.

Rule 1:13

> Similarly the enemy acts like a false lover, insofar as he tries to remain secret and undetected. For such a scoundrel, speaking with evil intent and trying to seduce the daughter of a good father or the wife of a good husband, wants his words and solicitations to remain secret. But he is deeply displeased when the daughter reveals his deceitful words and evil design to her father, or the wife to her husband. For he easily infers that he cannot succeed in the design he began.
>
> In a similar manner, when the enemy of human nature turns his wiles and persuasions upon an upright person, he intends and desires them to be received and kept in secrecy. But when the person reveals them to his or her good confessor or some other spiritual person who understand the enemy's deceits and malice, he is grievously disappointed. For he quickly sees that he cannot succeed in the malicious project he began, because his manifest deceptions have been detected.[9]

Desolation's second trick is seduction and deceit. When a person is prepared, evil resorts to secrecy. In such a case, a Christian, usually under the guise of some false loyalty or intimacy, is persuaded to keep quiet about inner and/or outer movements. This technique is one common to clandestine lovers of all ages. It is also frequently used by organized religions under the rubric of loyalty. Inappropriate family or institutional secrets are telltale warnings of a deceitful spirit.

How is the Christian to work against this deceit? Ignatius suggests a twofold strategy. First, one must find a person who is mature in the ways of discernment. Second, one must be open with that person about all the movements in one's heart.

Both points are extremely important. Ignatius is not promoting opening one's heart to anyone indiscriminately. He is not saying that a person with a religious title is automatically a good person with whom one should share. If one goes to a confessor, that confessor should be a "good" confessor. If one goes to another Christian, that Christian should be a "spiritual person." The need to be prudent and selective in choosing someone with whom to share one's heart is something that should not be taken lightly. Indeed one should pray intensely before choosing this person.

Once one has a person with whom one can reveal the movements in one's soul, then one must truly be open with this person. The movement of desolation will encourage one to say everything but certain things. Sometimes one's heart will be confused with movements of sexual temptations that are embarrassing or disheartening. At other times desolation will strike at the core of one's insecurities. All these things must be revealed to a wise and competent person. Speaking to one's confidant shines light into dark territory. Often telling the dark secret vanquishes the hold of desolation within the soul.

❧ *Rule 1:14 Know Your Vulnerabilities* ❧

Ignatius' final strategy is becoming a familiar one. If one is to act successfully against desolation, one must know the weaknesses of one's own heart. He pictures an enemy walking around the castle of one's life trying to find the weakest part of the wall.

Rule 1:14

> To use still another comparison, the enemy acts like a military commander who is attempting to conquer and plunder his objective. The captain and leader of an army on campaign sets up his camp,

studies the strength and structure of a fortress, and then attacks at its weakest point.

In the same way, the enemy of human nature prowls around and from every side probes all our theological, cardinal, and moral virtues. Then at the point where he finds us weakest and most in need in regard to our eternal salvation, there he attacks and tries to take us.[10]

Rule 1:14 harkens back to Rule 1:1. One must know one's weaknesses—where one is apt to go from bad to worse. One must be in touch with the strengths and weaknesses of one's personality and also with the current movements, desires, inclinations, passions and tendencies that are within and around one.

The movement of evil might even use one's own defense to instigate a further blow. For example, one may find oneself a victim of gossip. One counters the gossip by deciding to move against this desolation first, by praying for the one who is gossiping and secondly, by doing something good for him or her. The movement of evil might use this very goodness and tempt one with an attitude of superiority or a false sense of victimization. If one has moved contrary to desolation and this contrary movement within one's heart gradually moves into an overstatement or understatement, there are grounds for believing that evil is attacking the very place where one believes oneself to be strongest.

Summary

When one finds oneself tepid, sad or disillusioned with the Christian life, Ignatius advises one to strategize carefully and work against this desolation. The idea is to move contrary to the desolation. In order to move contrary one must do all one can to know oneself and to be in touch with the current movements, inclinations, desires and tendencies within and around one.

The time of desolation is not a time for making new decisions. Rather it is a time for holding fast to the decisions made during better days. One does all one can to counter desolation. Sometimes the only way to do this is to choose to persevere patiently in faith, hope and love. This perseverance can strengthen one's resolve and one's love for God and neighbor. One can be encouraged that God will always give one sufficient grace to overcome any desolation that God permits.

Movement against desolation is best done in a bold, confident style. Evil furiously attacks those it perceives to be weak. It is best to arm oneself with the power of God and to do one's best to persevere in moving contrary to desolation. This counter movement may require prayer, fasting and almsgiving, or rest, relaxation, recreation and time with friends. The key is not to fit oneself into some kind of stereotypical holiness regime, but to pay attention to one's own heart doing what is needed to invite a balance that can best foster healthy relationships with God, others and the world.

Finding someone who is wise and mature in the spiritual life and who has a gift for confidentiality is helpful since one is often blind to one's own weakness. Exposing the darkest corners of one's heart to a wise and prudent person sheds light upon the darkness of evil and exposes its secrets.

Moving against desolation gradually leads one to a balance and a joy that can be trusted by others. Desolation can be used as an instrument of purification, a sort of exercise by which one can strengthen one's desire and aptitude for the Christian life.

Rules 1:5-14
Strategizing the Blues

- **Rule 1:5 Keep Things Stable**
  Do not make new decisions during times of desolation.

- **Rule 1:6 Change Yourself**
  Counter desolation through prayer, self-examination and penance.

- **Rule 1:7 Prove Yourself**
  Use desolation as an opportunity to exercise your faith and to grow in self-knowledge.

- **Rule 1:8 Strive to Be Patient**
  Persevere in faith, hope and love.

- **Rule 1:9 Identify the Cause of Desolation**
  Name the root of your desolation. Ignatius offers three possibilities:
  (1) Negligence or tepidity in prayer
  (2) The grace to strengthen one's love for God in trial
  (3) The grace of learning by experience that consolation cannot be manipulated.

- **Rule 1:10 Prepare for Desolation**
  During times of consolation, prepare for desolation.

- **Rule 1:11 Move Toward Balance**
  During times of consolation and desolation, try to maintain balance by moving contrary to the primary movement.

- **Rule 1:12 Be Bold**
  Be dauntless when confronted by evil, arming yourself with Christ's strength.

- **Rule 1:13 Bring Secrets Into the Light**
  Reveal secrets hidden under the guise of false loyalty or intimacy to a wise and competent person.

- **Rule 1:14 Know Your Vulnerabilities**
  Examine yourself daily to know where you are weak and strong.

Case Study: Henry

Henry has been a loyal member of St. Andrew parish for the last 25 years. Because of his responsible service during these years, the pastor and a number of parishioners have asked Henry to submit his name as a candidate for parish council.

Henry is reluctant, but when he prays about the possibility of serving on the parish council, he experiences both great peace and also a deep sense of mission. A number of those returning to the council have a sense of social concern toward those who are poor in the parish, but they lack leadership and creative imagination. Therefore, in spite of their good will, social action has not been strong in the parish. Henry, a retired social worker, has a sense of what needs to be done and how to do it. When he prays, he feels a call to serve.

On Sunday, names of those on the ballot for the parish council are published in the parish bulletin. Mrs. Amery reads Henry's name and is indignant. Years ago, while working for social services, Henry mistakenly questioned whether the bruises on one of Mrs. Amery's children might have been caused by child abuse. Mrs. Amery has never forgiven Henry for his mistake. She starts a telephone campaign in the parish, telling people her story and accusing Henry of many things.

Henry is in a dilemma. On the one hand, he is receiving many secondhand reports of Mrs. Amery's accusations. He wonders if Mrs. Amery's campaign will render his candidacy useless and he is seriously considering withdrawing his name from the ballot. He has called Mrs. Amery, but she refuses to speak with him. On the other hand, he does feel a strong call to serve on the council. Those on the parish council are hoping for his appointment, and the other candidates do not possess the kind of leadership and vision that the council is looking for. Respecting your Christian perseverance and wisdom, Henry comes to you and wonders what he should do.

Questions For Reflection/Discussion

1. What are Henry's strengths in regard to this incident? How are the spirits working on these strengths?

2. What are Henry's "hooks" in regard to this incident? How are the spirits working on these weaknesses?"

3. Name the movements of consolation and desolation that you see in this case.

4. Using Rules 1:5-14, how might Henry move against the desolation he is experiencing?

Case Study: Carmen

Carmen is a young Hispanic woman who with her husband has recently left Mexico, legally entered the U.S., and currently lives in San Antonio. She and her husband are raising four children and are struggling to earn a living. Her husband works the fields and often travels north in the summer in search of better wages. This leaves Carmen and the children alone for months at a time. As a young wife, Carmen finds this difficult.

Because of her poverty, Carmen seems to have few options. Her life consists of taking in laundry when she can find this kind of work and caring for the children. She spends a great deal of time in government offices applying for programs to assist the family with food and health care.

A group of Franciscans has opened a retreat and prayer center in the neighborhood. Carmen goes there often for devotions to Our Lady of Guadalupe and, occasionally, for spiritual counsel.

Lately Carmen has been very discouraged. Her husband has been gone for three months, and she is lonely.

Although her husband's family who lives in San Antonio is very supportive, Carmen feels as though she is an added burden to their already limited financial means. She has no money to go north to be with her husband. If she and the children go back to her home in Mexico, it will be difficult and perhaps impossible for her to earn enough to care for the children. When she tries to pray, she feels as if God has abandoned her. Her children watch commercials on TV and wonder why they cannot have the computer games that other children have. Although Carmen does everything possible to provide for her children, her primary struggle is to make sure they have enough to eat.

The children do not understand. Carmen wishes that she could make her children happy. She is sometimes so discouraged that she wonders if perhaps she is losing her faith. Maybe she has done something to deserve all this, but she does not know what she might have done.

Questions for Reflection/Discussion

1. If Carmen came to you for spiritual counsel, how would you use Ignatius' Rules 1:1-14 to encourage her?
2. Is there anything to discern in this case? Can the poor benefit from discernment of spirits or is discernment a luxury reserved to those with options?

Suggestions for Further Reading

Buckley, Michael J. "The Structure of the Rules for Discernment." In *The Way of Ignatius Loyola: Contemporary Approaches to the Spiritual Exercises*, 219-228. Edited by Philip Sheldrake, S.J. St. Louis: The Institute of Jesuit Sources, 1991. Buckley begins his article by exploring various ways, i.e., preternatural influences, thoughts, emotions, affections, etc., through which people have sought to discover the guidance of God in their lives. Buckley then examines the interdynamics of preternatural influences, the role of thoughts, and attractions of affectivity within the context of the first set of *Rules*.

Toner, Jules, S.J. "The Good Spirit in Time of Desolation, Rules I:5-14." In *A Commentary on Saint Ignatius' Rules for the Discernment of Spirits*, 145-210. St. Louis: The Institute of Jesuit Sources, 1982. Fr. Toner's commentary is the most thorough scholarly work on Rules 1:1-14 available in English.

8

It's Not Always What It Seems

One does not have to be a Christian long before realizing that good people sometimes do bad things. Since it is difficult to tempt good people into blatant wrongdoing, evil tempts them under the guise of good. Christians can find themselves judging others under the pretext of righteous living. They can undermine others, convinced that they know the true path. They can even kill under the pretext of protecting Christian values.

Case Study: The Christian Women Society

A group of women parishioners at St. Benedict the Moor congregation offer a barbecued rib dinner one Sunday a month during the summer. One member of the group, Alice, is a hard worker but is difficult to get along with. Whenever it is her turn to be part of the kitchen crew, the spirit turns negative. People see her coming and are tempted to turn the other way.

Wilma, on the other hand, is someone people enjoy working with. She is a good organizer and is dedicated to continuing the dinner. Wilma tends to comment occasionally under her breath about some of the women, especially about Alice whose brash personality she finds difficult to tolerate. Wilma works so hard and is generally such a good-intentioned person that few can fault her for her occasional remarks. Sometimes, the women find her comments quite humorous.

One Sunday, Alice becomes upset because the plates for the dinner are not in their ordinary place. Thinking that Alice had left the kitchen, Wilma begins to imitate Alice's tirade. Finding this amusing, the other women join in taking turns mocking Alice's speech and mannerisms.

Alice, who is searching through a cupboard trying to locate the plates, overhears the conversation. She slams the cupboard door, gives the women a piece of her mind and leaves the kitchen. She does not return.

Eventually, Wilma breaks the silence saying that if Alice were not so grumpy, people would be kinder to her. The other women agree. The dinner goes on as usual, but without Alice.

Rules for Unmasking the Deception of Good People

Both Alice and Wilma are generally good people. Alice's temperament is a little more difficult for some people to tolerate than Wilma's. Wilma, however, even though she is dedicated to God's work and God's people, tends to be judgmental and perhaps even a bit cruel.

Wilma and the other women attempt to justify their judgmentalism. Wilma and the others are not totally perfect and Alice is not totally bad. All personalities have their strengths and weaknesses. If Wilma is convinced she is a good person and as such has the right to judge others, then she is deceived by her very goodness. In fact, Wilma is a good person; in fact, she also has the tendency to be judgmental.

Wilma and the other women seem to negate their responsibility for Alice's alienation and place the blame for this alienation solely on Alice. While Alice's crabbiness needs to be confronted, Wilma and the others did not address this truth in a loving way. As a result, there is alienation and a pall hangs over the kitchen.

Ignatius' second set of *Rules* addresses itself to the deception of good people. Although Christians desire to do good to others, at times they are deceived and in fact hurt others. To do this, an opposing spirit often overstates Christian values regarding religious living, righteousness or moral conduct. It is helpful to understand how and where this deception can occur. By identifying the "angel of darkness that masquerades as an angel of light," Christians are better able to work against this spirit of deception.

❧ Rule 2:1 Distinguish the Spirits by Their Fruits ❧

The task of discernment is to perceive, in order that one might understand, so that one might know how to act. Once one has firmly decided to follow the direction of the Holy Spirit, then evil has one choice. Since the Christian will not be tempted by blatant evil, evil must disguise itself as good. Ignatius' second set of the *Rules for Discernment* deals specifically with how to uncover this disguise.

While a Good Spirit brings happiness and joy, it is characteristic of an opposing spirit to bring alienation and sadness.

Rule 2:1

It is characteristic of God and God's angels by the motions they cause, to give genuine happiness and spiritual joy, and thereby to banish any sadness and turmoil induced by the enemy.

It is characteristic of the enemy to fight against this happiness and spiritual consolation, by using specious reasonings, subtleties, and persistent deceits.[1]

Evil can work against happiness that is rooted in God by "specious reasonings, subtleties and persistent deceits."

Ignatius' second set of *Rules* confronts the strategy of an opposing spirit that attempts to hide under the cover of good.

People who truly desire to live a Christian life can be deceived. A spirit of evil attempts to exaggerate or understate good intentions. A mother, for example, becomes so interested in making quilts for the poor that she consequentially disregards the needs of her family. Although she is neglecting her primary responsibility, the Christian community might even give her an award for her selfless dedication. A husband might decide to spend an hour a day in prayer but is negligent in helping his children with their homework. Although he is to be commended for his desire for prayer, he is perhaps abdicating his parental responsibility. Evil uses the consolation the father receives from prayer for its own purposes. If the father pushes the call to prayer to extremes, he can jeopardize his relationship with his children. The deceits of evil will eventually be uncovered in the sour fruits they bear.

❧ Rules 2:2-3 Identify the Type of Consolation ❧

Ignatius identifies two types of consolation. One type is unexpected and unplanned. Julie is walking to work when suddenly she receives insight into God's forgiveness in her life. She reflects later that she was not praying or even thinking about God in any way. She was simply walking to work when suddenly she received insight. Over time this insight has a profound effect on her life.

This type of consolation happens occasionally in a Christian life.

Rule 2:2

Only God our Lord can give the soul consolation without a preceding cause. For it is the prerogative of the Creator alone to enter the soul, depart from it, and cause a motion in it which draws the person wholly into love of his Divine Majesty. By "without cause" I mean without any previous perception or understanding of some object by means of which the consolation just mentioned might have been stimulated, through the intermediate activity of the person's acts of understanding and willing.[2]

Consolation without a preceding cause is a gift of God. It cannot be manipulated or controlled. The element of playful surprise and the creativity of the new insight or direction give credibility to the experience. The ultimate test of whether the experience is real is if it bears good fruits in the person's life.

Ignatius recognizes that consolation usually has a preceding cause.

Rule 2:3

With or by means of a preceding cause, both the good angel and the evil angel are able to cause consolation in the soul, but for their contrary purposes. The good angel acts for the progress of the soul, that it may grow and rise from what is good to what is better. The evil angel works for the contrary purpose, that is, to entice the soul to his own damnable intention and malice.[3]

A Christian husband, Daniel, decides that daily scripture reading is helpful to him. He finds that when he spends time each day contemplating the life of Jesus, he is capable of acting more like Jesus both at work and at home. One day, in the midst of his prayer, Daniel is talking with the Lord about his present employment and feels a call to look for a new job.

Initially Daniel feels peace and a bit of excitement about his prayer experience. His consolation is with preceding cause because it occurred while Daniel was praying about his employment situation. It does not seem to come out of nowhere as with Julie. If the consolation is from the Holy Spirit, Daniel will gradually become more convinced of the rightness of finding another place of employment. If the consolation is not from God, Daniel might be tempted to overstate or understate the importance of his spiritual experience and may make a rash decision. With all consolation, prudence and discretion are trustworthy guides.

Once Daniel recognizes the consolation that stems from his prayer experience, how can he know if he should act on it? If consolation can come from either good or evil, how does one discern its source? Ignatius gives some advice on this dilemma in his final *Rules*.

❧ Rules 2:4-5 Carefully Examine the Entire Process ❦

An opposing spirit sometimes disguises itself as a Good Spirit in order to deceive:

Rule 2:4

> It is characteristic of the evil angel, who takes on the appearance of an angel of light, to enter by going along with the devout soul and then to come out by his own way with success for himself. This is, he brings good and holy thoughts attractive to such an upright person and then strives little by little to get his own way, by enticing the soul over to his own hidden deceits and evil intentions.[4]

Although an opposing spirit can deceive a good person by means of false empathy, its own inability to persevere in goodness eventually reveals its deception. As a result, those discerning need to watch not only the beginning movements in which an opposing spirit might masquerade as an angel of light, but also middle and end movements.

Rule 2:5

> We should pay close attention to the whole train of our thoughts. If the beginning, middle, and end are all good and tend to what is wholly good, it is a sign of the good angel. But if the train of the thoughts which a spirit causes ends up in something evil or diverting, or in something less good than what the soul was originally proposing to do; or further, if it weakens, disquiets, or disturbs the soul, by robbing it of the peace, tranquility, and quiet which it enjoyed earlier, all this is a clear sign that it comes from the evil spirit, the enemy of our progress and eternal salvation.[5]

Discernment is not a skill that simply sorts through life's complications, providing one with clear and easy solutions. Rather, discernment is a task and a gift that one uses in daily life. Discernment does not provide Christians with immediate answers, but with a means to discover ways to grow in relationship with God, others and creation.

A person who wishes to be discerning needs to live a reflective life. A discerning lifestyle invites one to take time daily to ponder the direction of one's life and to identify the inner and outer movements that are affecting one. At times sorting through these movements is hard work, and the neophyte might wonder as Ignatius did in the beginning of his conversion: "What new life is this that we are now beginning?"[6]

Evil can begin by masquerading as consolation, but eventually the strain of goodness will be too much for it to sustain. It is fortunate for human beings that sloth and lack of perseverance are part of evil's deficiencies. False goodness will gradually betray its disguise. On the contrary, if a movement is of the Holy Spirit, its beginning, middle and end will consistently promote loving relationships with God, others and the world.

In discerning the beginning, middle and end of a consolation, one needs to check not only one's thinking but also one's heart and spirit. Sometimes one's head agrees with an idea, but one's intuition is not comfortable. The Holy Spirit brings balance to the whole human person. Before acting it is good to wait for peace.

All of this can lead one to think that discernment is hard work and perhaps nothing more than a kind of spiritual hypochondria. Ignatius' *Rules* attempt to exhort one not to discouragement but to a reflective life. By observing the beginning, the middle and the end, one begins to walk through life looking for signs of God's presence. Discernment awakens one's heart and mind to be ever attuned to the movements of God. Perfection is not required, only fidelity in one's relationship with God, others and the world.

❧ Rule 2:6 Learn from Mistakes ❧

Christians are bound to make mistakes in their struggles to develop discerning lifestyles. Ignatius, learning from his own experience, is aware of this and so provides guidance as to what to do when one discovers that one has been deceived.

Rule 2:6

> When the enemy of human nature has been perceived and recognized by his serpent's tail and the evil end to which he is leading, a new procedure becomes profitable for the person who was tempted in this way. He or she should examine immediately the whole train of the good thoughts which the evil spirit brought to the soul, including their beginning, and then how little by little the

evil spirit endeavored to bring the soul down from the sweetness and spiritual joy in which it had been, and finally brought it to his evil intention. Thus the person, by understanding this experience and taking note of it, can be on guard in the future against these characteristic snares.[7]

Finding that one has been deceived by an evil spirit is not an irreparable tragedy. Ignatius suggests that such an experience can even turn into grace. When one has uncovered deception, one has the opportunity to learn how evil gained entrance. This reflection may bring one to a greater depth of self-knowledge. Did the negative movement enter through one's strength or one's weakness? Did it begin as a consolation or as a sadness? Did it originate under the guise of a good but end in confusion?[8]

This type of examination can help one gain wisdom to guide one's future discerning. Even when it appears that the Christian has been deceived, there is the opportunity to learn from the experience. Christians can thus be grateful for everything, even their own weaknesses.

❧ Rule 2:7 Notice Harmonious and Discordant Spirits ❧

God is courteous. Any movement that barges into one's heart, thoughts or prayer in a discourteous way cannot be from God.

Rule 2:7

> In the case of those going from good to better, the good angel touches the soul gently, lightly, and sweetly, like a drop of water going into a sponge. The evil spirit touches it sharply, with noise and disturbance, like a drop of water falling onto a stone.

In the case of those who are going from bad to worse, these spirits touch the souls in the opposite way. The reason for this is the fact that the disposition of the soul is either similar to or different from the respective spirits who are entering. When the soul is different, they enter with perceptible noise and are quickly noticed. When the soul is similar, they enter silently, like those who go into their own house by an open door.[9]

This *Rule* harkens back to Rule 1:1. When a Good Spirit touches one where one is mature, there is harmony and peace. If evil tries to challenge one's maturity, there is discord. When a Good Spirit tends to one's area of weakness, pain and discomfort result. An opposing spirit will encourage one to be unreflective concerning one's weakness.

When one experiences desolation, one first discerns whether the confusion stems from a personal strength or weakness. A teacher, for example, might be effective in the classroom but may find it hard to take direction from the school's administration. If she discovers herself frustrated and discouraged, she might first wish to reflect on whether the desolation revolves around working with her students or around her dealings with the administration. If the desolation stems from her dealings with the administration, she might do well to examine herself closely. Choosing to write off the administration, believing in its incompetence and inadequacy, might provide her with a temporary feeling of superiority but will ultimately leave her in desolation. Challenging her extreme attitudes toward the administration might be initially more painful but, in the end, may yield consolation. Perhaps not all the administrators are incompetent and inadequate. Acknowledging the administration's strengths might improve her spirits and help her see how changes can be made. Perhaps refraining from her quick judgments might yield a more creative and fruitful approach.

All this requires a great deal of mature honesty. It is easy to get caught in patterns of quick judgment and righteous legitimizing. The Holy Spirit will challenge these patterns of darkness, and will, of necessity, cause pain when doing so.

The pain occasioned by the encouragement of the Holy Spirit, however, and the pain caused by evil are different. The pain allowed by the Holy Spirit invites a better, happier future; the pain of evil promotes apathy and violence. The pain of the Holy Spirit works for one's growth and betterment, while the pain of evil has no regard for the one being hurt.

ᴥ *Rule 2:8 Discern the Afterglow* ᴥ

After one has experienced consolation, one is often prompted to do some kind of good action in the afterglow of this consolation. This is a laudable movement but must be carefully discerned. Not all action, even that which may seem praiseworthy, is necessarily inspired by God.

Rule 2:8

> When the consolation is without a preceding cause, no deception can be present in it, since it is coming only from God our Lord, as was stated above. However, the spiritual person to whom God gives this consolation ought with great vigilance and attention to examine his or her experience as to distinguish the time when the consolation itself was present from the time after it, in which the soul remains still warm and favored with the gifts and aftereffects of the consolation which has itself passed away. For very often during this later period the person, through either his or her own reasoning which springs from one's own habits and from conclusions reached by one's own con-

cepts and judgments, or through the influence of either an angel or a devil, forms various proposals and convictions which are not coming immediately from God our Lord. Hence these need to be very carefully examined before they are fully accepted or carried into effect.[10]

Consolation that is without previous cause is immune to deception because its direct source is God. An evil spirit can act upon it only after the direct consolation has passed. Julie received insight into God's forgiveness while walking to work one day. The spontaneity and creativity of the inspiration seem to mark it as coming from God. How she will put this inspiration into action concretely, however, still needs to be carefully discerned. Perhaps she should see Aunt Jane and tell her that she can finally forgive her. Perhaps she should take more regular time for prayer to allow the grace of God's forgiveness to move more deeply in her. Perhaps, since she no longer needs so much energy to foster bitterness, she can now do some volunteer work.

Julie's experience of God's forgiveness gives her insight but there is still much to be discerned. Consolation without previous cause may inspire new direction, but it does not negate the necessity of continuing discernment.

Summary

It is difficult to persuade a committed Christian to choose that which is blatantly evil. Good people do, however, fail in their love toward God, neighbor and the world. Christians are often deceived by that which appears good but proves to be destructive of loving relationships.

Even when consolation seems to come directly from God, it is wise to discern carefully choices made after this consolation. Often the spirit of evil will move in after such consolation, attempting to deceive under the pretext of faith or generosity.

Such deception can be uncovered when Christians live reflective lives. Evil masquerading as good cannot persevere in its awkward disguise. One who is reflective notices when an evil disguised as a good stumbles over its true nature. Those who examine the inroads of deception are less likely to be vulnerable to the same mistakes in the future. One grows in discernment by prayerfully reflecting on both the consolations and desolations in one's life.

Rules 2:1-8
Unmasking the Deception of Good People

- **Rule 2:1 Distinguish the Spirits by Their Fruits**
  Observe the fruits of the movements.

- **Rules 2:2-3 Identify the Type of Consolation**
  Identify whether or not the consolation has a preceding cause.

- **Rules 2:4-5 Uncover Deception**
  Reflect upon the beginning, middle and end of a discernment process.

- **Rule 2:6 Learn from Mistakes**
  Examine your train of thoughts to identify where you were deceived.

- **Rule 2:7 Notice Harmonious and Discordant Spirits**
  Identify whether the movement is acting upon your strength or weakness and then whether the movement is harmonious or discordant.

- **Rule 2:8 Discern the Afterglow**
  Any new directions proceeding from the afterglow of a consolation without previous cause must be carefully discerned.

Case Study: Ramona

Shortly after their marriage, Ramona and her husband move to a small town where they join the local parish. Ramona had been active in her former parish especially in the youth group and in music ministry and eagerly anticipates a similar involvement in her new parish community.

After a few weeks in her new parish, Ramona is somewhat disappointed. Her pastor leads an unspirited half-hour Sunday liturgy with virtually no participation. The parishioners are intelligent, but they do not seem to be frustrated by the pastor's style.

Ramona continues to be faithful to daily reading of the Scriptures and to prayer and finds joy in doing this. She wants to find others in her new parish community who are interested in sharing faith and prayer.

Always ready for a challenge, Ramona asks the pastor if she might begin a Bible discussion group. She also volunteers to organize readers for the Sunday liturgy. Ramona feels like she is responding well to a situation that might have discouraged other women with her pastoral skills. When she thinks about the contribution she can make to her new parish, she begins to experience happiness and hope.

Over time, despite Ramona's best efforts, the people in her new parish show little interest in either Bible discussion or organized reading. Undaunted, Ramona initiates a Thursday night Bible study during her second year in the parish. She has it well organized and promotes the study after Sunday services. On Thursday night, no one comes. Ramona feels alone and alienated.

Questions for Reflection/Discussion

1. Ramona initially seemed so encouraged about her ministry to the people in her new parish. What went wrong?
2. Apply Rules 2:1-8 to this case.

3. Can you think of times in your life when you felt you were doing something positive and you ended up in desolation? How might Rules 2:1-8 be helpful in reflecting upon your situation?

Case Study: Jerry

Jerry is a man who is faithful to prayer and comes regularly to a retreat center in Milwaukee's inner city. He is mentally ill and is in treatment through the County Mental Health Center. He began coming to the retreat center to talk to someone who could help him sort out who God is in his life.

Right now medication keeps the mental illness stable. Jerry feels good about this stability and appreciates the fact that he is well enough to enjoy life.

Jerry goes to St. George church every day and spends an hour in private prayer. He enjoys praying the stations and looking at the windows that depict different Gospel stories. Occasionally he also picks up the scriptures, but the windows are the primary source of his consolation in prayer.

Jerry looks forward to his appointments for spiritual direction. His director notices Jerry's faithfulness to prayer and the profound depth of his prayer.

Lately, however, Jerry is becoming more and more angry with the system. He is tired of having to wait in long food lines that serve macaroni and little meat. He is annoyed with living from government check to government check.

Because of his illness, Jerry's employment record has been sporadic, and social workers cannot convince another employer to take the risk of hiring Jerry. Jerry shakes as a side effect of his medication and is walking with more and more difficulty. Finding a job does not seem to be a realistic possibility. Jerry often feels rejected by others, and the inability to be hired for a job intensifies this feeling of rejection.

In spiritual direction Jerry shares that he feels Jesus is
with him and that Jesus talks with him. When his spiritual
director asks what Jesus says, Jerry cannot remember exactly. The words obviously are not important to Jerry.
Jerry just enjoys sitting with Jesus and listening. Jerry also
tells Jesus what he thinks about things in prayer. Sometimes when he feels frustrated, Jerry tells Jesus that he is
going to stop praying until Jesus finds him a job.

Question for Reflection/Discussion

If you were Jerry's spiritual director, how would you
use the *Rules for Discernment* in working with him?

Suggestions for Further Study

Buckley, Michael J. "The Structure of the Rules for Discernment." In *The Way of Ignatius Loyola: Contemporary Approaches
to the Spiritual Exercises*, 228-237. Edited by Philip Sheldrake,
S.J. St. Louis: The Institute of Jesuit Sources, 1991. In his
commentary on the second set of the *Rules*, Buckley explores
the relationship between rational intentionality and affectivity.

Lonsdale, David. "'The Serpent's Tail': Rules for Discernment." In *The Way of Ignatius Loyola: Contemporary Approaches to the Spiritual Exercises*, ed. Philip Sheldrake, S.J.,
165-175. St. Louis, MO: The Institute of Jesuit Sources, 1991.
Lonsdale explores the possibility of good people being deceived by false goods and offers practical examples to illustrate various ways this deception might occur.

Toner, Jules, S.J. "Deception Beginning in Spiritual Consolation: Rules II:1-7" and "Deception During the Afterglow of
Spiritual Consolation: Rule II:8." In *A Commentary on Saint
Ignatius' Rules for the Discernment of Spirits*, 213-256. St.
Louis: The Institute of Jesuit Sources, 1982. In these chapters, Toner outlines the Ignatian *Rules* concerning deception
during times of consolation.

Epilogue

Falling in Love
with the Holy Spirit

Discernment is a loving vigilance toward God, others and the world that seeks to do the truth in love. It is an art rather than an answer. It is a dance that moves through the vicissitudes of life in a way that grounds love in truth and truth in love.

The gift of discernment is given to those who gradually fall in love with the Spirit of God. The Holy Spirit is a practical Spirit who moves throughout one's days and within one's relationships.

Discernment of the movements that affect one's life and relationships begins by noticing what is happening in one's inner and outer worlds, so that one might understand the direction of the Spirit of God. One understands inner and outer movements when one distinguishes those movements that are of the Holy Spirit from those that might turn one away from loving relationships with God, others and the world.

Understanding, however, is not the end of discernment. Love shows itself in deeds (1 Jn 3:18). Those who identify which movements in life tend toward true and loving relationships with God and others are better able to choose appropriate action.

Persons who move in the direction of true and loving relationships gradually grow in their ability to do the truth in love. As one matures in discernment, one's love of the Spirit of God experienced in everyday relationships grows more intimate.

One who desires intimacy with the Spirit of God needs to counter movements that are not from the Holy Spirit. These movements are characterized by confusion, apathy, indecision and mistrust. One counters the opposing spirit with boldness exposing its secrecy by prudently and courageously bringing its darkness into the light.

The presence or lack of presence of the Holy Spirit is discerned not only by reflecting upon desolation, but also in assessing one's strengths. Deception often occurs when people consider themselves strong. In these cases, an opposing spirit can mimic a Good Spirit for a time, but will be unable to persevere in its disguise. The reflective person must constantly be alert even when all seems rooted in God. One who is in love with the Holy Spirit of God and seeks to follow the movements of the Spirit in the midst of everyday life, soon learns that one must be vigilant in both consolation and desolation (1 Pet 5:8-9).

Those maturing in discernment find themselves experiencing a foundational peace that is not easily undermined by the ups and downs of daily life. They learn to choose consistently a spirit of truth and love even when they encounter desolation. These Christians speak and live in a way that invites the communion of God, human persons and creation. Although they might be persecuted and sometimes even killed for their words and for the example of their lives, Christians who love the Spirit of God inspire the hearts of others to persevere in doing the truth and to proclaim the truth lovingly.

"The fruit of the Spirit is love, joy, peace, patience, kindness, generosity, faithfulness, gentleness and self-control" (Gal 5:22). Those who are in love with the Holy Spirit begin to radiate the Spirit's fruits. Even if they are misunderstood or maligned, those who love the Spirit respond with an intelligence and a wisdom that speaks the truth while tenderly respecting the other.

Those who fall in love with the Holy Spirit of God find joy. Their prayerful response is praise, awe and gratitude.

Their demeanor is peace, courage and gentleness. Their passion is love grounded in truth.

Discernment is a gift and a task. In the midst of responsibly developing the gift of discernment, one who desires Trinitarian communion through the Spirit of God in the midst of daily life needs to pray for the fullness of this gift. Without the grace of discernment given in prayer, all discernment skills and processes are useless. If one desires discernment, one must practice a discerning lifestyle and beg God fervently and humbly for this gift.

Notes

Chapter One

1. In his introduction to "The Spiritual Exercises," St. Ignatius states: "I must make myself indifferent to all created things, in regard to everything which is left to my freedom of will and is not forbidden. Consequently, on my own part I ought not to seek health rather than sickness, wealth rather than poverty, honor rather than dishonor, a long life rather than a short one, and so on in all matters" [23]. The translation used in this text is taken from "The Spiritual Exercises" in *Ignatius of Loyola: Spiritual Exercises and Selected Works*, ed. George E. Ganss, S.J. (New York: Paulist Press, 1991).

2. For a review of the necessity of detachment in the spiritual life see *The New Dictionary of Catholic Spirituality*, 1993 ed., s.v. "Detachment," by George E. Ganss, S.J.

3. For example, St. Benedict's Rule states: "The reason why we have said all should be called for counsel is that the Lord often reveals what is better to the younger" [3:3]. See *The Rule of St. Benedict*, ed., Timothy Fry, O.S.B. (Collegeville, MN: The Liturgical Press, 1981). St. Clare copies Benedict's prescription and inserts it into her own Rule substituting the word "least" for "youngest." Her admonition thus reads, "for the Lord frequently reveals what is best to the least" [4:13]. See the "Form of Life of Clare of Assisi," ed. and trans. Regis J. Armstrong, O.F.M. Cap. (St. Bonaventure, N.Y.: Franciscan Institute Publications, 1993).

4. George Tavard states: "If tradition is memory, it is living, not archival memory" in "Vatican II, Understood and Misunderstood," *One in Christ* 27 (1991), 211.

5. Those who object to the central principle of incarnational theology that God indwells the world have from the beginning been refuted by orthodox Christians. The early Christian heresies of Gnosticism, Marcionism, Docetism and Arianism all supported beliefs that God could not inhabit an evil world. Christianity has consistently rejected this tenet insisting that matter is good precisely because it is created, indwelt and transcended by the good God. For further reflection on the early Christian struggle regarding the deification of the cosmos see Louis Bouyer, *Cosmos: The World and the Glory of God* (Petersham, MA: St. Bedes Publications, 1988), 97-107. To avoid

the error of pantheism, Christians hold that God's presence in the world is mediated. For further discussion on this point see Karl Rahner, *Foundations of Christian Faith* (New York: The Seabury Press, 1978), 81-89.

Chapter Two

1. For further reading on cultic criticism in the book of Amos see Klaus Koch, *The Prophets: The Assyrian Period* (Philadelphia: Fortress Press, 1989), 50-66.

2. For further study on Israel's discernment in regard to true and false prophets see Martin McNamara, "Discernment Criteria in Israel: True and False Prophets," in *Discernment of the Spirit and of Spirits*, ed. Casiano Floristán and Christian Duquoc (New York: The Seabury Press, 1979), 3-13, and Walter Vogels, "Comment discerner le prophète authentique?," *Nouvelle Revue Théologique* 99 (1977): 681-701.

Chapter Three

1. Survey studies on discernment in the Christian tradition include Jacques Guillet, Gustave Bardy, Francois Vandenbrouchke, Joseph Pegon and Henri Martin, *Discernment of Spirits*, trans. Sister Innocentia Richards (Collegeville, MN: The Liturgical Press, 1970), and my own article, "The Theology of Discernment: A New Historical Overview," *Studies in Formative Spirituality* XII (February 1991): 105-118.

2. John of the Cross, *The Collected Works of St. John of the Cross*, trans. Kieran Kavanaugh, O.C.D. and Otillo Rodriguez, O.C.D. (Washington D.C.: Institute of Carmelite Studies, 1964), 683-84.

3. C.S. Lewis, *The Screwtape Letters* (New York: Macmillan Publishing Co., Inc., 1978), 30-31.

4. Athanasius, *The Life of Antony and the Letter to Marcellinus*, trans. Robert C. Gregg (New York: Paulist Press, 1980), 58-59.

5. *Little Flowers of Saint Francis*, trans. Raphael Brown, in *St. Francis of Assisi: Writings and Early Biographies*, ed. Marion Habig (Chicago: Franciscan Herald Press, 1973), 1334-35.

6. For a contemporary story that relates the choice of a Franciscan woman to involve friends in her discernment process see, Margaret Halaska, OSF, "A Model of Discernment: The Experience of a Franciscan," *Review for Religious* (March/April, 1984): 259-63.

7. Teresa, "With God and a Medical Kit in the Mountains," in *El Salvador: A Spring Whose Waters Never Run Dry*, ed. Scott Wright, Minor Sinclair, Margaret Lyle and David Scott (Washington, D.C.: Ecumenical Program on Central America and the Caribbean, 1990), 36-37.

8. Although Ignatius synthesizes many elements of the Christian spiritual tradition, it does not seem that he composed the "Rules for Discernment" with this purpose. The "Rules for Discernment" flow from his lived experience of relating with God. On the other hand, Ignatius was enculturated within the Christian tradition and was influenced by this tradition. For comment on the influence of the patristic and monastic traditions on the writings of Ignatius see Joseph T. Lienhard, S.J., "On 'Discernment of Spirits' in the Early Church," *Theological Studies* 41 (Sept. 1980): 506-507.

Chapter Four

1. A brief sketch of Ignatius' life with one example from his "Autobiography" is given here. Those who wish to explore further the theme of discernment in Ignatius' "Autobiography" may find it helpful to consult Harvey D. Egan, S.J.'s outline in *Ignatius Loyola the Mystic*, The Way of Christian Mystics Series, vol. 5 (Wilmington, DE: Michael Glazier, 1987): 146-48.

2. "Autobiography," [7-8]. The translation used in this text is taken from Ignatius of Loyola, "The Autobiography," in *Ignatius of Loyola: Spiritual Exercises and Selected Works*.

3. For further discussion concerning belief in the spirit world and its implications on discernment see, Jules J. Toner, S.J., "The Existence of Satan and Demons: Theological Opinions on It as an Object of Christian Belief," in *A Commentary on Saint Ignatius' Rules for the Discernment of Spirits* (St. Louis: The Institute of Jesuit Sources, 1982), 260-270.

4. "The Spiritual Exercises," [313].

5. Ignatius of Loyola, "The Spiritual Exercises," [24-26].

6. An explanation of the similarities and differences of spiritual direction and counseling and the role of these services in helping a person become more self-reflective can be found in Maureen Conroy, R.S.M., *Growing in Love and Freedom* (New Jersey: Dimension Books, 1987).

Chapter Five

1. Mortal sin could be referring here to the traditional capital sins of pride, sloth, gluttony, lust, anger, avarice and envy. Mortal sin in this sense refers to strong personal tendencies which have the capacity to lead one away from true and loving relationship. As used in this context, these weaknesses are not great crimes in themselves but are problematic because they have the potential of eroding one's moral fiber. For further discussion on this point see Toner, *A Commentary on Saint Ignatius' Rules for the Discernment of Spirits* (St. Louis: The Institute of Jesuit Sources, 1982), 50-51.

2. "The Spiritual Exercises," [314].

3. Jules Toner, S.J., distinguishes Ignatius' pedagogical method of presenting "pure cases" from the concrete complexities of human life. Toner uses the example of the rich young man (Mark 10:17-22) to illustrate the effect of the spirits on an otherwise maturing individual whose weakness is called into play. Unless one realizes that each person is in some sense both maturing and regressing, one is faced with a simplistic notion of the *Rules* that offers little enlightenment when dealing with human complexity. For further discussion on this point see Toner, *A Commentary on Saint Ignatius' Rules for the Discernment of Spirits*, 70-78 and 205-206.

4. "The Spiritual Exercises," [315].

Chapter Six

1. "The Spiritual Exercises," [316].

2. For further reflection see my own article, "The Theme of Joy in the *Spiritual Exercises*," *Review for Religious* 49 (March/April 1990): 283-88.

3. This theme echoes the spiritual teachings of Julian of Norwich. See *Julian of Norwich: Showings*, trans. Edmund Colledge, O.S.A. and James Walsh, S.J. (New York: Paulist Press, 1978), 225.

4. "True and Perfect Joy," in *Francis and Clare: The Complete Works*, trans. Regis J. Armstrong, O.F.M. and Ignatius C. Brady, O.F.M. (New York: Paulist Press, 1982), 165-66.

5. "The Spiritual Exercises," [317].

Chapter Seven

1. "The Spiritual Exercises," [318].

2. Ibid., [319].
3. Ibid., [320].
4. Ibid., [321].
5. Ibid., [322].
6. Ibid., [323].
7. Ibid., [324].
8. Ibid., [325].
9. Ibid., [326].
10. Ibid., [327].

Chapter Eight

1. "The Spiritual Exercises," [329].
2. Ibid., [330].
3. Ibid., [331].
4. Ibid., [332].
5. Ibid., [333].
6. Ignatius of Loyola, "Autobiography" [21].
7. "The Spiritual Exercises," [334].
8. Further reflection and examples regarding deception during times of consolation can be found in David Lonsdale, "'The Serpent's Tail': Rules for Discernment," in *The Way of Ignatius Loyola*, ed. Philip Sheldrake, S.J. (St. Louis, The Institute of Jesuit Sources: 1991), 165-75.
9. "The Spiritual Exercises," [335].
10. Ibid., [336].